The Cathedral and Leaning Tower, Pisa, Italy

The
WONDERS
of the
WORLD

Prepared by
The Book Division
National Geographic Society
Washington, D.C.

The WONDERS of the WORLD

Contributing Authors Leslie Allen, Stephen L. Harris, Catherine Herbert Howell, K. M. Kostyal, Rick Sammon

Published by The National Geographic Society
John M. Fahey, Jr. **President and Chief Executive Officer**
Gilbert M. Grosvenor **Chairman of the Board**
Nina D. Hoffman **Senior Vice President**

Prepared by The Book Division
William R. Gray **Vice President and Director**
Charles Kogod **Assistant Director**
Barbara A. Payne **Editorial Director and Managing Editor**
David Griffin **Design Director**

STAFF FOR THIS BOOK
Bonnie S. Lawrence **Project Editor and Senior Researcher**
Carolinda E. Hill **Text Editor**
Thomas B. Powell III **Illustrations Editor**
Lyle Rosbotham **Art Director**
Kimberly A. Kostyal **Researcher**
Alicia Moyer **Research Assistant**
Carl Mehler **Senior Map Editor**
Jehan Aziz **Map Production**
Bonnie S. Lawrence, Peyton H. Moss, Jr. **Contributing Writers**
Richard S. Wain **Production Project Manager**
Lewis R. Bassford **Production**
Meredith C. Wilcox **Illustrations Assistant**
Peggy Candore, Kevin G. Craig, Dale-Marie Herring **Staff Assistants**

MANUFACTURING AND QUALITY CONTROL
George V. White **Director**
John T. Dunn **Associate Director**
Vincent P. Ryan **Manager**
Polly P. Tompkins **Executive Assistant**

Mark A. Wentling **Indexer**

Previous Pages: The Pyramids, Giza, Egypt; opposite: Golden Gate Bridge, San Francisco, U.S.A.

CONTENTS

....

Opposite: Grand Canyon, U.S.A.

Wonders never cease, nor does our eternal fascination with them. We delight in encountering marvels that astonish us with their extraordinary size, beauty, or strangeness. For in their presence we are transported out of our routine-controlled lives and brought face-to-face with things that command awe, admiration, or even reverence.

These are the emotions that seem to have stirred Herodotus in the mid-fifth century B.C. An indefatigable traveler, as well as the "father of history," he wrote home enthusiastically about the world's amazing sights, letting his fellow Greeks know how exciting travel could be.

The Greeks' desire to see and hear about awe-inspiring works of art and architecture received a powerful boost about a century after Herodotus, when Alexander the Great conquered most of the known world. Alexander's empire, extending from Greece to India, spawned a prosperous new era in which trade and tourism flourished. Greek writers almost immediately began compiling inventories of attractions that no traveler could afford to miss. Although different authors, including Antipater of Sidon and Philo of Byzantium, produced varying tallies, eventually there emerged a standard catalogue of marvels, known today as the Seven Wonders of the Ancient World.

The canonical seven—two tombs, two statues, a temple, a garden, and a lighthouse—shared an important quality: their tremendous size. Viewers also were impressed by their aesthetic splendor, the technological skill of their builders, and the sheer daring of their conception.

Why seven? For the ancient world, the number signified perfection or completion. The sum of four and three, even and odd, female and male, it symbolized cosmic wholeness. Although the lists of wonders changed significantly over time, the selections always totaled seven.

A WORLD OF WONDERS

· · · · · · · · · ·

by Stephen L. Harris

After the Colosseum's dedication in A.D. 80, the poet Martial called the structure a new world wonder. It remains an enduring monument to Rome's imperial glory.

Ancient Wonders

Pyramids of Giza
Hanging Gardens of Babylon
Temple of Artemis at Ephesus
Statue of Zeus at Olympia
Mausoleum at Halicarnassus
Colossus of Rhodes
Pharos of Alexandria

Medieval Wonders

Stonehenge
Colosseum
Catacombs of Kom el Shoqafa
Great Wall
Porcelain Tower of Nanjing
Hagia Sophia
Leaning Tower of Pisa

Natural Wonders

Mount Everest
Great Barrier Reef
Grand Canyon
Victoria Falls
Harbor of Rio de Janeiro
Paricutín Volcano
Northern Lights

Underwater Wonders

Palau
Belize Barrier Reef
Galápagos Islands
Northern Red Sea
Lake Baikal
Great Barrier Reef
Deep-Sea Vents

Modern Wonders

Empire State Building
Itaipú Dam
CN Tower
Panama Canal
Channel Tunnel
North Sea Protection Works
Golden Gate Bridge

30°W   0°   30°E   60°   90°   120°   150°

Northern Lights

Lake Baikal

ASIA

North Sea Protection Works

Stonehenge

Channel Tunnel

EUROPE

Leaning Tower of Pisa

Colosseum

Hagia Sophia

Great Wall

Temple of Artemis at Ephesus

Statue of Zeus at Olympia

Mausoleum at Halicarnassus

Porcelain Tower of Nanjing

Colossus of Rhodes

Deep-Sea Vent

Hanging Gardens of Babylon

Mount Everest

Pharos of Alexandria

Pyramids of Giza

Catacombs of Kom el Shoqafa

Northern Red Sea

AFRICA

Pacific Ocean

Palau

Indian Ocean

Victoria Falls

Great Barrier Reef

AUSTRALIA

0   2000 mi

0   3000 km

ANTARCTICA

By the time classical civilization declined in the late fifth century A.D., the concept of Seven Wonders had become thoroughly ingrained in the Western consciousness. Even after the Greco-Roman world lay in ruins, medieval churchmen such as Gregory, the Bishop of Tours, and Bede, a scholarly English monk, perpetuated the idea by compiling new lists that reflected changed historical conditions. Gregory's list, the first-known compilation to include the Pharos—lighthouse—of Alexandria, is typical of his period, mixing items from Philo's ancient inventory with two Judeo-Christian marvels: Noah's Ark and Solomon's Temple.

Gregory also encouraged his readers to revere the daily miracles by which God administers the universe. Earth's real wonders, he believed, could be seen in the motions of the sun, moon, and tides; in the germination of seeds; and in the spectacular eruptions of volcanoes.

In his monastery at Jarrow, England, the Venerable Bede drew up an even more eclectic list of wonders. Perhaps the most bizarre item was "the iron statue of Bellerophon on his horse." He claimed the mythical Greek hero's statue was suspended in air by means of two huge magnets. Needless to say, this airborne wonder, allegedly weighing 5,000 pounds, existed only in Bede's uncritical employment of unreliable sources.

During the Renaissance, European artists and scholars cultivated a passionate interest in antiquity, producing not only new lists of wonders but, for the first time, illustrations of how they imagined them to have appeared. In the late 1500s, Dutch artist Maerten van Heemskerck created a series of drawings that showed the Seven Wonders of the Ancient World. His numerous imitators included Maerten de Vos, who pictured the Colossus standing astride the harbor of Rhodes, an image that, while inaccurate, remains indelibly imprinted on the popular imagination.

As natural as the act of breathing, the impulse to seek out and enumerate works that move and delight us characterizes each generation. We prepare new inventories of the marvels by which we take the measure of our cultures. From the graceful bridge arching across San Francisco's Golden Gate to Australia's Great Barrier Reef, the largest living organism, a world of wonders reminds us of our essential humanity. And like the Greeks who first assessed the quest for immortal achievements, we remain poised between our ambition to dominate nature and our awareness of nature's inevitable victory.

Seen through the mist on England's Salisbury Plain, the ancient sacred site known as Stonehenge evokes the mystery of a lost prehistoric culture that endured for 1,600 years.

The big, the bold, and the beautiful—these were the qualities distinguishing the buildings and statues that Hellenistic writers put on their lists of the ancient world's Seven Wonders.

The Greek historian Herodotus started the trend of praising gigantic structures in the fifth century B.C., but the custom of taking inventories of "must-see" landmarks did not get under way until after the conquests by Alexander the Great. The international culture that Alexander created, a fusion of Greek and older Near Eastern civilizations, spawned a new self-awareness among Hellenistic peoples, who were eager to exploit the commercial potential, including tourism, of Alexander's far-flung empire.

Among the first to publish a list of wonders was Callimachus of Cyrene, a noted scholar at the Library of Alexandria in Egypt. In the third century B.C., he wrote *A Collection of Wonders in Lands Throughout the World*. Although his work is now lost, it inspired a host of imitators, including Antipater, a Greek author from the Phoenician city of Sidon, and Philo of Byzantium, whose surviving inventories name six of the Seven Wonders that ultimately became canonical. (Instead of the Pharos, a lighthouse at Alexandria, Philo and Antipater mention the walls of Babylon, which Herodotus said were 56 miles in circumference.)

Five of the traditional seven—the Temple of Artemis at Ephesus, the Statue of Zeus at Olympia, the Mausoleum at Halicarnassus, the Colossus of Rhodes, and the Pharos of Alexandria—are of Greek origin. The remaining two, Giza's Pyramids and Babylon's Hanging Gardens, were also contained in Alexander's empire. In making their choices, Hellenistic writers clearly intended to promote the glories of Greek culture. "The list which we have inherited," one modern author remarks, "is a fragment of ancient advertising."

SEVEN WONDERS of the ANCIENT WORLD

....

by Stephen L. Harris

Greeting the morning sun for more than 4,500 years, the three Pyramids of Giza—oldest and sole surviving wonder of the ancient world—seem as ageless as the desert sands surrounding them.

The Pyramids of Giza

· · · · · · · · · ·

Ancient Wonders

Workers at Giza hauled limestone
blocks along a stone causeway linking
a Nile canal with the building site.
Gleaming sheaths of polished rock
encased the completed structures.

Nothing in his native Greece had prepared Herodotus for the Great Pyramid looming above him on Egypt's Giza plateau. Awestruck by its vast bulk, height, and antiquity, the Greek historian marveled at the almost inconceivable amount of labor that must have been needed to build it.

When Herodotus visited Egypt about 450 B.C., Khufu's 481-foot-high tomb was already more than 2,000 years old, but he had no trouble collecting stories about its origin. To this champion of the Athenian democracy and to many later visitors from the Greco-Roman world, the Great Pyramid was the work of a tyrannical egomaniac. Even in his day, Herodotus said, the Egyptians still hated Khufu and Khafre, the pharaohs responsible for the two largest pyramids, and could "hardly bring themselves to mention [their] names."

Herodotus's informants told him that Khufu had enslaved Egypt's people to erect this monument to his vanity, working a hundred thousand men "in three monthly shifts" for ten years just to build the track used for hauling huge stones to the construction site. The same number of slave laborers took 20 more years to build the Great Pyramid itself, which contains 2.3 million limestone blocks weighing an average of 2.5 tons apiece.

With an eye for humanizing detail, Herodotus also reported that his interpreter had translated an inscription recording the amount of money Khufu expended to supply "radishes, onions, and leeks for the labourers." It added up to 1,600 talents, a fabulous sum equivalent to several million dollars today. "If this is true," Herodotus wondered, "how much more must have been spent in addition on bread and clothing" for the workers?

Visitors in the classical period were awed by the phenomenal time, expense, and effort involved in constructing what is still the world's largest stone building. Modern visitors are equally impressed by the immensity and accuracy of all three of Giza's giant structures. Trying to explain how they were constructed, a few people have even suggested that the ancient Egyptians, whose rudimentary technology relied on rollers and levers, could not have built them without extraterrestrial help.

Khufu's Great Pyramid (opposite) dwarfs lesser tombs clustered at its base, a square precisely aligned with the four points of the compass.

Climbers follow a local boy up the giant staircase of Khafre's Pyramid (left), still capped with a remnant of its original limestone veneer.

Only three inches tall, the seated ivory figure of Khufu (above) represents the only known portrait of the king who built Egypt's largest pyramid.

Although today's archaeologists and engineers do not entirely agree on whether the Egyptians used encircling ramps, scaffolding, rollers and levers, or other methods, they do concur that the architects and engineers did not need advanced technology from outer space. The political power of the early pharaohs and the even more powerful ideas they represented were enough to bring the pyramids into being.

In the society of the Old Kingdom, which produced the gigantic structures at Giza during a 75-year period (circa 2585 to 2510 B.C.), the pharaoh was not only the supreme head of state but also the figure who linked the immortal world of the gods with the human realm. Alive, he embodied Horus, the god of light; deceased, he was identified with Horus's father, Osiris, lord and judge of the dead. By the 26th century B.C., the pharaoh had also become associated with Re, god of the sun.

The Great Pyramid bears the Egyptian name *Akhet-Khufu*, the "horizon of Khufu," indicating that it marked the place where the deified ruler appeared each day as the sun. The shape of the pyramid, with its apex piercing the sky, symbolized a titanic beam of the sun god's life-giving light and warmth, frozen in stone to provide a stairway for the pharaoh's soul to rise heavenward. As the eternal shelter for the pharaoh's body, Khufu's Pyramid offered his people reassuring evidence of their king's posthumous immortality and his continuing power to influence the gods on their behalf. Rather than a symbol of regal oppression, the pyramid was designed to express a visible link between heaven and earth.

When Herodotus and other travelers of the Greco-Roman period saw it, Khufu's memorial was not only overwhelmingly huge but also a work of breathtaking beauty, its exterior walls entirely sheathed in polished white limestone. Philo of Byzantium reported that the outer casing was "joined together so seamlessly that it seems to be made out of one continuous rock," a gleaming model of geometric perfection. Like many of antiquity's great edifices, Khufu's tomb served later cultures as an easily accessible stone quarry, and its glossy covering was stripped away to furnish building material for medieval Cairo. Today, only a fragment of the pyramids' formerly smooth surfaces remains: a weathered remnant at the apex of Khafre's monument.

Although no tomb builder has been more successful in perpetuating his name than Khufu, it is ironic that no trace of his mummy remains and that only one tiny figurine survives to preserve his likeness. Khufu's tomb suffered from the depredations of grave robbers who probably rifled his sarcophagus during one of the political upheavals that punctuate Egyptian history.

Despite the passage of time and the ravages that were inflicted by later despoilers, Khufu's memorial still dominates the Nile's west bank south of Cairo, a rock-solid testimony to the creative force of an idea. Percy Bysshe Shelley, an English poet who lived in the early 19th century, intended to disparage such grandiose exploits when he wrote, "look on my works, ye Mighty, and despair." But in the case of Khufu's accomplishment, Shelley's ironic jab at a forgotten despot does not apply. Considering the 46 centuries that the pyramids have endured, an Arabic proverb is closer to the mark: "Man fears time, but time fears the pyramids."

At Giza, Egypt, the Pyramids of Menkaure, Khafre, and Khufu (left to right) stand as enduring monuments to the ancient civilization that created them.

The Hanging Gardens of Babylon

....

Ancient Wonders

Encircled by impregnable walls and maintained by water from the River Euphrates, Babylon's fabled gardens created a luxurious oasis amid the bleak Mesopotamian desert.

Elusive as a desert mirage and as tempting as Eden's forbidden fruit, the legendary Hanging Gardens of Babylon evoke images of a lost paradise. A lush, perfumed oasis amid the arid, flat plain surrounding the queen city of the ancient Near East, the gardens rose in densely planted tiers to form an artificial mountain of greenery within Babylon's mighty walls.

Philo of Byzantium, in the third century B.C., placed the gardens first on his wonders list, pinpointing the quality that made them wonderful: They defied nature. In a parched, featureless landscape, people had created what nature had not—an extravagance of shade trees, colorful flowers, luscious fruits, and splashing fountains. As if to emphasize their artificiality, the gardens were "hanging," rooted on lofty terraces that, as Philo noted, "[suspended] the work of cultivation over the heads of spectators."

The impulse to break natural law by fashioning this botanical marvel was said to derive from a king's love for a woman. According to Berossus, a Babylonian priest or scholar who wrote a history of Mesopotamia for Greek readers, the builder was Nebuchadnezzar II (605-562 B.C.). The most powerful monarch of the Neo-Babylonian Empire, Nebuchadnezzar constructed the gardens to please his Median wife, who had become homesick for the forested mountains of her native land.

About 50 B.C., Diodorus Siculus, a Sicilian-Greek historian, wrote that the multileveled gardens were supported

With a horned viper's head, a lion's front legs, and a bird of prey's hind legs, this scaly-coated dragon—fashioned in glazed-brick relief—symbolizes Marduk, creator of the universe and chief god of Babylon.

by a complex structure of thick brick walls, stone pillars, and closely spaced beams made from palm tree trunks. To make the supporting edifice watertight, the palm beams were overlaid with mats of reeds and bitumen, as well as two layers of baked mud bricks, all covered in a veneer of lead. Water to irrigate the vegetation was pumped from the nearby Euphrates River, probably by slave labor. The astonishing result was a cool, humid, scented oasis that was fit for gods and which has delighted the Western imagination ever since.

Of all the Seven Wonders, however, only the gardens left no evidence that they ever existed. Although modern archaeologists have thoroughly excavated Babylon, they have not found a structure that fits the descriptions given by Hellenistic authors. Several possible sites have been proposed, such as a large vaulted edifice uncovered by the German archaeologist Robert Koldewey in the early 1900s, but none has yet won general acceptance by scholars. Particularly damaging to the notion of the gardens' reality is the fact that none of the thousands of cuneiform texts found at Babylon, including an inventory of the city's monuments, ever mentions them. The historian Herodotus, who strongly implies that he visited Babylon in the fifth century B.C., is equally silent.

By contrast, portions of Babylon's huge defensive walls—so broad that "four-horse chariots [could] easily pass one another" along the top, according to the Greek geographer Strabo—remain solidly in place. Cited by Philo as a wonder in themselves, the walls were partly rebuilt in the 1980s by Iraq's Saddam Hussein, who had planned to make Babylon a mecca for tourists.

Although the gardens' actual existence has not been confirmed, there is nothing inherently improbable about the concept. From remote antiquity, Mesopotamian kings adorned their cities with lavish green areas. Gilgamesh,

Before the Persian Gulf War in 1991, Iraq's Saddam Hussein began to rebuild the walls of ancient Babylon (right), an ambitious project designed to attract tourists from around the world.

In a bas-relief (below) from Ashurbanipal's palace at Nineveh, musicians perform in a royal garden.

the legendary king of Uruk, reportedly laid out a third of his capital in gardens. Even the Assyrian rulers, who were widely feared for their savagery against opponents, were dedicated gardeners. Ashurnasirpal II, for example, flayed captured enemies alive, but he was also an avid plant collector who embellished Nimrud with rare trees, shrubs, and flowers in the ninth century B.C.

Descriptions of Ashurnasirpal's landscaping efforts indicate that he erected high walls to hold in moisture from streams and waterfalls, which in turn required elevated areas sufficient to provide a gradient for irrigation channels: "The canal water comes flowing down from above to the gardens: the paths are full of scent; the waterfalls glisten like the stars of heaven in the garden of pleasure. The pomegranate trees are clothed with clusters of fruit like vines, and enrich the breezes in the garden of delights. Ashurnasirpal gathers fruit continuously in the garden of joys...."

The Mesopotamian rulers' penchant for redesigning nature to suit their whims, as well as their military successes against smaller states such as Israel, earned them a bad reputation in the Bible. Western views about Babylon have been partly shaped by biblical stories about Nebuchadnezzar, who in 587 B.C. sacked Jerusalem, destroyed Solomon's Temple, and deported the upper classes to Babylon.

Decorated with blue glazed tiles, the reconstructed Ishtar Gate on display at the Berlin Museum honors Babylon's volatile goddess of love and war. The gate's low-relief sculptures of sacred dragons and bulls symbolize divine power.

According to the Book of Daniel, Nebuchadnezzar then dared to boast about the magnificence of his capital: "Great Babylon! Imperial palace! Was it not built by me alone, by my own might and power to the glory of my majesty?" Daniel wrote that the ruler's pride met with swift punishment by God, who stripped Nebuchadnezzar of his reason and condemned him to live like a wild beast for seven years.

Although Babylonian archives do not substantiate Daniel's claim that Nebuchadnezzar suffered from insanity at any point during his 43-year reign, archaeological excavations reveal that he was indeed one of the Near East's greatest builders. Nebuchadnezzar finished the construction of the enormous walls, built the encircling moat that formed a formidable barrier to would-be invaders, and rebuilt most of central Babylon, transforming it into an urban wonder that Herodotus said "[surpassed] in splendour any city of the known world."

Among Nebuchadnezzar's achievements was the Ishtar Gate, with its bas-reliefs and blue enameled tile facing. Dedicated to the goddess of love and war, the gate stood along a processional avenue where Babylonian armies once marched to commemorate the triumphs of their chief god, Marduk, creator of heaven and earth.

Alexander must have passed through Ishtar's portals when he entered Nebuchadnezzar's former capital, the final stop in his series of military campaigns. Perhaps, as he lay dying there, the 32-year-old world conqueror gazed at the Hanging Gardens, seeing in their ephemeral beauty the promise of a more enduring paradise.

The Temple of Artemis at Ephesus

....

Ancient Wonders

With its "forest" of glistening marble columns, the Temple of Artemis at Ephesus dazzled viewers as a vision of the gods' celestial habitation gloriously materialized on the earth.

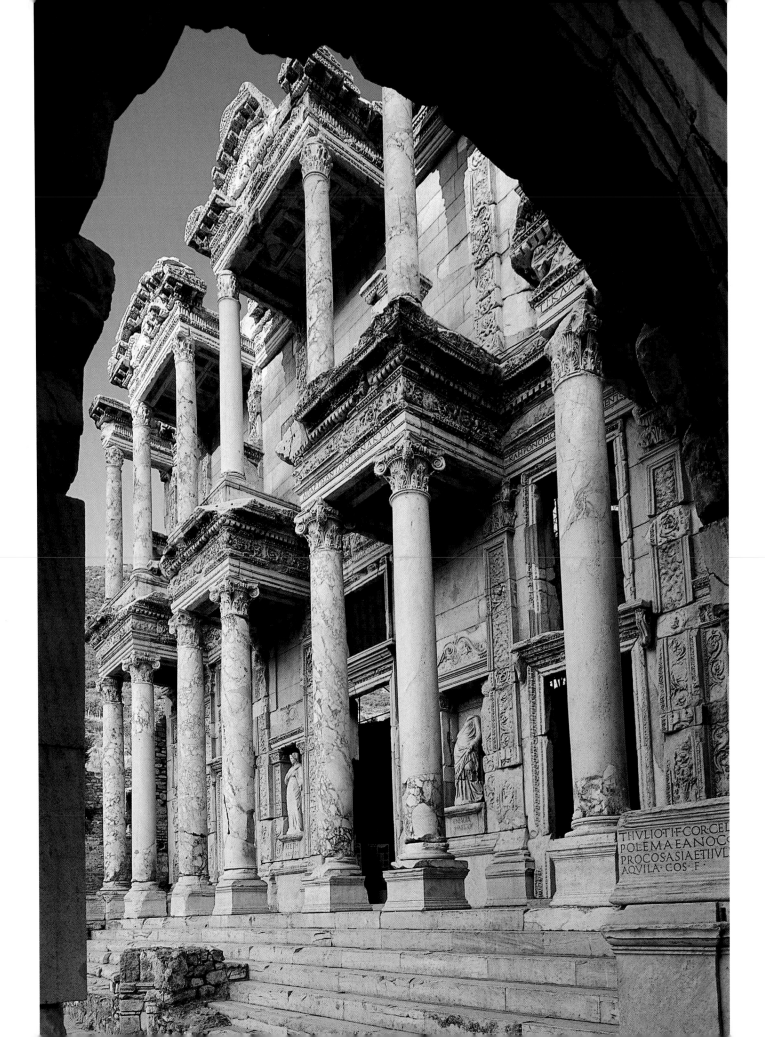

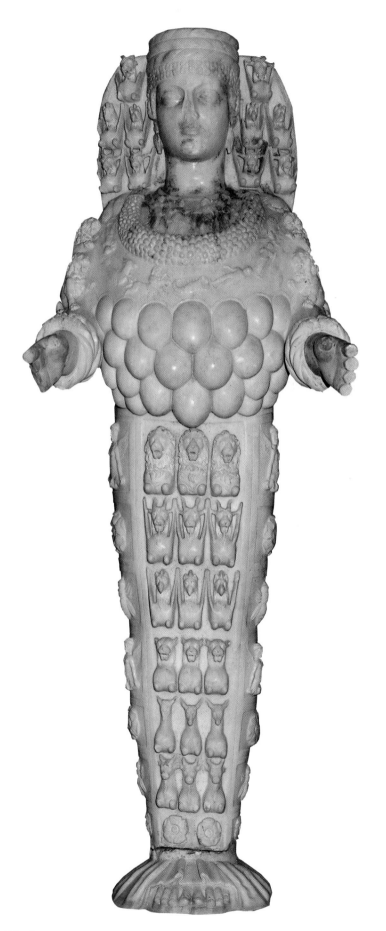

Renowned for their love of luxury and display, the citizens of Ephesus, wealthiest seaport in Asia Minor, staged annual processions to honor Artemis—the goddess whose enormous marble temple was one of the world's Seven Wonders. Gorgeous apparel, bright colors, clouds of incense, and joyful music marked the celebrations of Artemis's birthday in late May, when under clear, azure skies the deity's image was paraded through the city.

Democritus of Ephesus proudly described his fellow citizens' sense of fashion: Some participants wore Ionian robes "dyed violet, purple, and yellow...decorated at equal intervals with pictures of animals." Others were arrayed in Corinthian styles of "crimson...flame-orange or sea-green." Still others chose expensive Persian robes spangled with gold beads attached to purple cords.

A deity who inspired passionate devotion and luxurious festivals, Artemis (Diana, to the Romans) was the daughter of Zeus and twin sister of Apollo, god of music, poetry, health, and prophecy. A paradoxical figure, she was both a virgin and the guardian of childbirth; benign protector of wildlife, she was also patron of the hunt. The Artemis worshiped at Ephesus, though, was much different from the slim huntress shown in the art of mainland Greece. Surviving copies of her cult statue seem bizarre, almost grotesque. The original appears to have been a stiff column decorated with animal heads up to the waist, culminating in a mass of protuberances variously identified as breasts, eggs, fruits, or the testicles of bulls sacrificed on her altar. Except for the head and extended arms, this Artemis reveals few human features.

Archaeological excavations show that Artemis's devotees had made offerings at the site of her sanctuary long before Croesus, the fabulously wealthy king of Lydia, built her first great temple in the sixth century B.C. Designed by a Cretan architect, Chersiphron, the temple combined a Greek rectangular floor plan measuring 375 feet by 180 feet with an Egyptian hypostyle hall. A "forest" of fluted Ionic columns stood in rows two deep around the central sanctuary, with 14 pairs along each side and 6 along each end. The structure also featured a

Wealthy and sophisticated, Ephesus boasted many works of architectural distinction, including the Library of Celsus (opposite), its two-story facade adorned with elegant porticoes.

Artemis's cult statue (right)—decorated with heads of lions, bulls, and deer, and bearing multiple breasts, fruits, or perhaps the testicles of bulls—reveals a stylistic kinship with Asiatic fertility goddesses.

Life-size figures embellish a marble column drum (above), the best-preserved sculpture from the late classical Temple of Artemis. Centuries ago, admirers praised the quality of the temple's many sculptures.

Ancient Ephesus's theater (right) once witnessed celebrations in honor of Artemis and a riot led by silversmiths fearful of the Apostle Paul's teachings.

central passageway of columns connecting the vestibule with the inner cell housing Artemis's cult statue.

In 356 B.C., allegedly on the day of Alexander's birth, a maniac named Herostratus set the temple on fire, gutting the entire shrine. Reconstruction was already under way in 334 B.C., when Alexander stopped at Ephesus early in his conquest of Persia. The young king offered to sponsor the rebuilding, but Artemis's priest reportedly declined the offer by saying that it was unsuitable for one god to honor another. Whatever the truth of this exchange, Alexander subsequently dispatched his own architect, Dinocrates, to supervise the project.

The new structure surpassed its predecessor not only in size but also in the quality of its art, with sculptors and painters competing to produce the most gorgeously decorated shrine in the Hellenistic world. As the Roman Pliny the Elder remarked in the first century A.D., the temple compelled "real admiration for Greek magnificence." Even the Romans, who prided themselves on the huge

scale of their public buildings, were forced to concede that the Greeks had set a standard difficult to emulate.

The second temple was erected on a nine-foot-high platform accessible by ten wide marble steps. With its white forest of 127 gleaming columns, each 60 feet tall, and its doors and supports decorated in gold and bright paints, Artemis's temple dominated the harbor and drew all eyes as mariners approached the shore. Seeing the magnificent temple gave admirers a good idea of how the

gods' celestial dwelling place must have appeared. As Philo of Byzantium remarked, the sanctuary brought "the heavenly world of immortality...[down to] the earth."

On a less spiritual plane, many Ephesian artisans reaped large profits by fashioning miniature replicas of the goddess's shrine and selling them to tourists, but this popular enterprise was threatened when the Apostle Paul visited Ephesus during the mid-50s A.D. According to the Book of Acts, Paul's preaching against idolatry infuriated

Bearing an image of Artemis's temple, a bronze coin (above) issued during the reign of Caesar Maximus (A.D. 235-238) helps archaeologists reconstruct the building's appearance. Capped by a stork's nest, a solitary column rising above a field littered with marble fragments (right) now marks the site of the Greco-Roman world's most magnificent sanctuary.

a local silversmith named Demetrius, who, along with other craftsmen fearing a loss of their incomes, incited a riot in the theater. Ultimately the silversmith's objections to the new faith proved prophetic: If Christian views prevailed, "the temple of the great goddess Artemis will be scorned, and she will be deprived of her majesty that brought all Asia and the world to worship her."

In A.D. 262, a Gothic horde sweeping down from the Crimea attacked Ephesus and destroyed Artemis's sanctuary. Despite the devastation, Ephesus recovered and rebuilt the shrine so essential to its economic well-being. But this structure would not stand long. After it was damaged by a fourth-century earthquake, it fell victim to the zeal of a new religion. The Patriarch of Constantinople, in A.D. 401, ordered an assault that plundered the goddess's treasury and stripped her sanctuary of its art. Limekilns were set up to melt down the remaining marble into mortar, while the building was quarried, block by block, to furnish stones for new churches, roads, and fortifications.

Having suffered from earthquakes, invasions, demolition crews, and gradual burial under silt from the River Caÿster, Artemis's shrine is no more. A single battered column, raised by modern archaeologists and topped by a stork's nest, now marks the place where the feminine principle of divinity was joyfully adored for millennia.

The Statue of Zeus at Olympia

....

Ancient Wonders

Made of ivory and gold, Phidias's 40-foot-tall statue of Zeus dominates its Olympian shrine. At Zeus's feet, a pool of olive oil reflects the Greek god's awe-inspiring image.

Excitement ran at fever pitch when crowds gathered at Olympia to witness the most famous athletic competitions of antiquity and to urge their favorites on to victory. Drawing the finest athletes from city-states all over the Greek world, the Olympic Games featured grueling contests in running, jumping, wrestling, and boxing, as well as races for chariots and single horses.

The games honored Zeus, king of the Olympian gods, whose great temple dominated Olympia's sacred precincts. According to tradition, the competition was founded in 776 B.C. by Hercules, the mythical hero famous for his strength, or by Pelops, who was said to have defeated his prospective father-in-law, Oenomaus, in a chariot race. Scheduled in late summer, the games were a force for Greek unity and a major religious event. Custom demanded that military hostilities cease when heralds announced the upcoming games every four years. During the five-day festival, a hundred oxen were sacrificed at Zeus's altar and a solemn ceremony was held in which athletes swore to obey the rules of the games. The festivities opened with a procession from Elis, the nearby host city, and ended with enthusiastic celebrations.

About 438 B.C. the Council of Olympia commissioned the Athenian sculptor Phidias to create a gigantic statue of Zeus. A close friend of Pericles, the leader of the Athenian democracy, Phidias had already produced two heroic statues of Athena, the goddess of wisdom for whom Athens was named. One was an enormous bronze statue of the goddess holding her characteristic warrior's spear and shield. It stood atop the Acropolis, the high hill on which Pericles had built Athena's most famous temple, the Parthenon. This bronze goddess literally dazzled: Sunlight flashing from Athena's helmet crest and spear point could be seen from far out at sea. The other statue, nearly 40 feet high and draped in a ton of gold, was housed inside the Parthenon, so called because it was dedicated to Athena Parthenos—the Virgin.

In constructing his representations of Athena and Zeus, Phidias employed a process known as chryselephantine, a method by which a wooden frame is overlaid with closely joined panels of ivory for the flesh and gold for the garments. The completed statues were lavishly decorated in jewels, silver, copper, enamel, glass, and paint, creating likenesses of divinity that were both colorful and radiant. Although the statues have long since vanished, descriptions of their splendor survive in works by several Greek and Roman authors.

Pausanias, who traveled in Greece during the second century A.D. and catalogued its shrines and monuments, detailed the embellishments with which Phidias had depicted Zeus's diverse attributes. Embodying natural forces and ethical principles, Zeus was a god of the heavens, manifested in thunder and lightning, and also the enforcer of justice, civic order, and hospitality:

"There is a garland on his head made as if of olive shoots. In his right hand he is carrying a Victory [the figure of Nike, a personification of victory], also made of gold and ivory, and this figure is holding a ribbon and has a wreath on its head. In the left hand of the god is a sceptre decorated with every kind of precious metal. The bird perched on the sceptre is the eagle [symbol of Zeus's rulership of the skies]. The sandals of the god are made of gold too, and so is his robe. Embroidered on the robe are figures of animals and white lilies. The crown is ornate with its gold and jewels, ornate with its ebony and ivory."

Seated on his throne, Zeus loomed 40 feet above the observer, filling the temple with his presence. At Zeus's feet was a large, shallow pool of olive oil

that kept visitors from approaching the statue too closely. It reflected sunlight from the temple doorway onto Zeus's face (otherwise it would have been obscured by shadows in the windowless sanctuary) and may have provided moisture to keep Zeus's ivory skin from drying out.

Philo of Byzantium clearly understood the sense of divinity evoked by the statue: "Whereas we just wonder at the other six wonders, we kneel in front of this one in reverence, because the execution of the skill is as incredible as the image of Zeus is holy...." Numerous classical writers echoed Philo's view that in fashioning his image of supreme majesty, giving shape to an ineffable ideal, Phidias had achieved a vision unmatched by other artists.

Not every visitor was uncritically impressed by Phidias's accomplishment, however. With a scientist's practicality, the geographer Strabo observed that if Zeus

Black figures race across an orange background on a vase (left) depicting an Olympic event. The games also held competitions in jumping, boxing, wrestling, and chariot racing.

Portraying Zeus seated in his shrine, the carving on a carnelian ring (above) illustrates a theoretical difficulty with Phidias's statue: If the god stood up, his head would go through the roof.

Sculptors decorated Zeus's temple with a frieze depicting the 12 labors of Hercules, the god's mortal son. In this scene (below), Hercules holds up the sky, while Atlas returns with golden apples from the Hesperides.

To honor Zeus, whose Doric sanctuary appears at the center of this model (above), Olympia hosted Greece's foremost athletic contests every four years.

Excavating the site of Zeus's Olympian temple,
19th-century archaeologists found the sanctuary
a jumble of toppled columns (above). Earthquakes,
Christian despoilers, and sediment from the River
Alpheus had obliterated the shrine.

This statue of Zeus's son Apollo (right), who per-
sonified reason, health, and manly beauty, originally
occupied the west pediment of Zeus's temple.

were to stand up, his head would go through the temple's
disproportionately low roof. Even more skeptical, the
Roman satirist Lucian compared the hollow statue's hidden scaffolding—infested with rats and mice, he said—to
the inferior reality lurking behind the grandiose images
that kings and emperors presented to the public.

Severely damaged and then repaired after an earthquake in 170 B.C., Zeus's temple and cult statue suffered
even greater blows when Christianity became the official
religion of the Roman Empire. Emperor Constantine
decreed that gold was to be removed from pagan shrines,
an order that probably resulted in Phidias's statues being
stripped down to their wood and ivory components. In
A.D. 393 the emperor Theodosius abolished the Olympic

Games, ending a tradition that would not be revived for 15 centuries. One of Theodosius's court officials was a eunuch named Lausus. An ardent collector of classical art, he appropriated what remained of Zeus's statue and transported it to his private gallery in Constantinople. Historians believe that the remnants of Phidias's master-work probably were consumed in the fire that swept the city in A.D. 475 or were destroyed in riots in 532.

Although ostensibly vanquished by the new religion, Phidias's image of Zeus was reborn in portraits adorning

Although little remains of its former splendor, Olympia still attracts tourists eager to view the ancient place where athletic contests provided inspiration for today's international competitions.

Orthodox churches in the Byzantine Empire. Mosaics and paintings of Christ sitting in judgment exhibit the same straight nose, centrally parted hair, flowing locks, and intense gaze with which an Athenian sculptor had long ago expressed his glimpse of the divine mystery.

Legend attributes the creation of antiquity's most lavishly decorated tomb, the Mausoleum at Halicarnassus, to a royal love affair. After the unexpected death of King Mausolus of Caria, a state on the coast of Asia Minor, his grief-stricken queen, Artemisia, built a memorial that would testify to her devotion. Even the unromantic writer Pliny the Elder was moved by the story: "This tomb was built for Mausolus, king of Caria, by his wife, Artemisia.... [The region's greatest] artists worked so hard on the work that it became one of the Seven Wonders.... Before they completed the project, the queen died. But they did not abandon the...work; already they saw it as a monument to their individual glory and skill...."

The fact that Artemisia, who was Mausolus's sister as well as his wife, died in 351 B.C., only two years after her brother-husband, suggests that the tomb was begun well before the king's demise. A structure as large and elaborate as the Mausoleum, with its scores of intricate sculptures, would have taken quite a long time to construct.

Composed about A.D. 75, Pliny's description is the most complete extant account. It emphasizes that the Mausoleum employed at least five of the Greek world's finest sculptors. Four were each assigned one of the structure's sides; each man competed to produce the most elegant carvings and statuary. According to Pliny, "the length of the North and South sides is sixty-three feet, the length of the front and back is less, the whole perimeter being four hundred and forty feet. Its height is forty feet and is surrounded by thirty-six columns. People called the surrounding colonnade 'pteron' [Greek for a wing]. Scopas carved on the east side, Bryaxis on the north, Timotheus on the south and Leochares on the west.... A fifth artist also entered the running. For above the pteron there is a pyramid of a height equal to the lower structure, and in twenty-four steps it tapers to a point. At the top there is a four-horse marble chariot which Pytheos made. Including the addition on top, the whole work is one hundred forty feet high."

Although Pliny is correct about the total height, he underestimates the building's dimensions (probably about 120 by 100 feet). The finished edifice, in shimmering white marble, stood at the intersection of two main streets in the city's center, soaring high above Halicarnassus's defensive walls. Backed by rugged hills and facing the azure sea, the Mausoleum seemed almost ethereal. A Roman poet noted that it looked as if it were "poised in empty air."

We do not know why Mausolus constructed such an elaborate tomb. Historians suggest that he wished to leave posterity a monument immortalizing his role as founder, the ruler who reestablished and rebuilt Halicarnassus as one of the eastern Mediterranean's most prosperous cities. In durability, the tomb outlasted all but one of the other ancient wonders, standing until it was deliberately torn down by European soldier-monks nearly 1,900 years later.

Although it was completed almost 20 years before Alexander captured Halicarnassus, the Mausoleum's creative mixture of architectural styles anticipated the eclecticism of the later Hellenistic era. A vivid example of cultural synthesis, the tomb's principal levels represented components of the Lycian, Greek, and Egyptian civilizations. The platform or base, which Pliny simply calls "the lower part," stood about 60 feet high and was modeled on traditional Lycian funereal architecture. Above this platform rose the second section, enclosed by rows of 36 graceful Ionic columns, each of which was nearly 40 feet tall. The steep pyramidal roof consisted of 24 marble steps tapering to a

The Mausoleum at Halicarnassus

....

Ancient Wonders

Hailed as the most magnificent funerary monument in the Aegean world, the Mausoleum integrated strikingly different architectural styles, including a Greek colonnade and a pyramidal roof.

flat platform at the apex and was perhaps 22 or 23 feet high. It was surmounted by a sculpture group featuring four marble horses, a chariot, and a driver—adding 20 feet to the total height.

The exquisite quality of its sculptures and the extraordinary way they were integrated into the structure made the Mausoleum truly wonderful in the eyes of Greco-Roman visitors. Unfortunately, nearly all of the few fragments that have been recovered from its ruins are badly damaged and relatively ordinary. Among the exceptions are two statues of a man and a woman, which are superb. The better preserved male figure, commonly and probably incorrectly identified as a portrait of King Mausolus, combines anatomical realism with a sensitive rendering of facial expression and character. If the more than one hundred larger-than-life-size statues adorning the tomb were of comparable quality, the Mausoleum would have displayed a throng of masterpieces.

Although the Mausoleum was damaged by an earthquake in the 13th century, most of the edifice was still standing in A.D. 1522, the year that it was ordered demolished. Father Sabba di Castiglione, a Christian monk then living on the nearby island of Rhodes, wrote that the Grand Master of the Knights Hospitaller "is naturally hostile to...antiquity." Like many others of their time, the Grand Master and his knights regarded pagan art as contaminated, even dangerous to the faith.

Ironically, the Mausoleum's best-preserved statuary—including a head commonly identified as Mausolus (opposite, top), a marble chariot horse wearing a bronze bridle (top left), and a figure often identified as Queen Artemisia (above)—toppled from the structure during an earthquake. Later buried in sediment, these pieces escaped melting by limekilns. The frieze showing a mythical battle scene between Greek soldiers and the Amazons (left) survived because locals used the marble slabs to cover a drain culvert.

Today, only a few scattered fragments of fluted columns and blocks of stone mark the site of the Mausoleum (above). Basking in Aegean sunlight, the modern city of Bodrum, Turkey, occupies the site of ancient Halicarnassus (right). A Crusader castle, built by the Knights Hospitaller in the 15th century and fortified in the 16th century by blocks from the tomb, looms above the harbor.

Needing material to fortify the Castle of St. Peter, near the little town of Bodrum, against an anticipated Turkish attack, the Knights Hospitaller found an easily accessible supply of stones in the Mausoleum, then partly buried in sediment washed down from the neighboring hills. Fortunately, some of the sculptured stones were added to the castle's walls as decoration and thus preserved.

Fifty years after the event, Lyonnais Claude Guichard wrote an account of how thoroughly the knights pulverized sculptures and melted them down to make mortar. He said that the knights dismantled the marble steps of the upper structure still standing above ground and then dug beneath the surface to uncover the central edifice:

"In a short time they saw that the deeper they went, the more the structure was enlarged, supplying them not only with stone for making lime, but also for building.

After four or five days, having laid bare a great space one afternoon, they saw an opening as into a cellar. Taking a candle, they let themselves down through this opening, and found that it led into a fine large square apartment, ornamented all round with columns of marble, with their bases, capitals, architrave, frieze, and cornices, engraved and sculptured in half-relief. The space between the columns was lined with slabs and bands of marbles of different colors, ornamented with mouldings and sculptures...and inserted in the white ground of the wall, where battle-scenes were represented sculptured in relief. Having at first admired these works...and...the singularity of the sculpture, they pulled it to pieces, and broke up the whole of it...."

Ironically, the much feared Turkish assault took place on Rhodes, not the site of Halicarnassus. The Knights Hospitaller quickly abandoned their last outpost in Asia Minor, but only after having razed this ancient wonder.

The Colossus of Rhodes

....

Ancient Wonders

Soaring 110 feet above its marble pedestal, a statue of the sun god Helios holds aloft a torch in this reconstruction of the Colossus. Legend says that Helios rescued Rhodes from invaders.

Radiating solar beams, the head of Helios on a silver coin issued by Rhodes in the third century B.C. depicts the city's patron deity and may represent the facial appearance of the Colossus (above).

At the Rhodes Museum, a marble head dating from the time of Lysippus immortalizes the face of Helios (left). Equidistant holes in the chiseled hair once held metal sunbeams streaming from Helios's head.

Ever since a 16th-century engraver showed the Colossus straddling Rhodes's harbor, this inaccurate image has held the popular imagination (opposite).

In the fourth century B.C., the sun god Helios was said to have delivered the people of Rhodes from a harrowing siege. To show gratitude to their patron, the Rhodians erected the Colossus, a gigantic bronze statue towering 110 feet above its marble base—more than two and a half times the height of Phidias's Olympian Zeus.

An embodiment of the all-seeing, all-nourishing sun, the Colossus expressed the essence of wonder. With its bronze skin reflecting sunlight, this vast figure of Helios must have bedazzled observers and created a persuasive image of the god. As Philo of Byzantium saw it, sculptor Chares of Lindos had achieved the miraculous, making his god visually "equal to *the* god." On this Aegean island, Chares had "set a second Helios [sun] facing the first."

To the citizens of Rhodes, the circumstances that led to the building of the Colossus were as miraculous as the statue itself. In 305 B.C., Antigonus, a Macedonian leader who hoped to take over the deceased Alexander's empire, sent his son Demetrius to punish Rhodes for its refusal to side with him against Ptolemy of Egypt. Former generals under Alexander, the two rivals competed for control of the Aegean Sea trade, a money-making venture at which Rhodes's merchant fleets were phenomenally successful.

Demetrius "the Besieger" sailed to Rhodes with 200 warships carrying 40,000 men, an intimidating contrast to the Rhodian forces of about 6,000 or 7,000. Employing a mobile siege tower some 150 feet tall and sheathed in iron plates, he battered the walls of the city relentlessly. Although their walls were breached, Rhodes's citizen-soldiers drove him back, forcing him to abandon his year-long attack and to accept a compromise peace. With their usual business acumen, the Rhodians sold the tower and other military scrap for a huge sum, using it to commemorate the god who had saved their lives and fortunes.

COLOSSVS SOLIS.

Chares, the artist-engineer commissioned to design and erect Helios's monument, was a pupil of Lysippus, the sculptor renowned for his lifelike portrait busts of Alexander. Although some historians suggest that Chares gave the Colossus Alexander's facial features, we know disappointingly little about the statue's exact appearance. Modern attempts at reconstructions are hindered by conflicting archaeological evidence. For example, many Hellenistic coins bearing the god's image incorporate conventional solar symbols, such as a crown of radiating spikes (solar rays) encircling his head, but some do not.

In 1932, a fragmented bas-relief showing the upper half of the body of Helios or Apollo was unearthed on Rhodes and used to reconstruct the statue's appearance. The sculpture depicted the god, complete with a solar halo, raising his right hand to shield his eyes and resting his left hand on his hip. But other scholars believe that Helios held his right arm aloft and brandished a flaming torch, a concept that influenced the pose for the Statue of Liberty. (The marble relief eventually was identified as an athlete crowning himself.)

Ideas about the god's lower body are also controversial. Like most statues of male Greek deities, Helios probably stood upright in glorious nudity, but did his great weight rest entirely on slim ankles? When constructed in New York Harbor during the late 19th century, the figure of Liberty was swathed in voluminous draperies that masked her lower extremities and helped to support her massive torso. Was the Colossus of Rhodes, although nude, similarly supported by a cloak that hung to the ground from his shoulder or arm?

One point on which scholars agree is that Chares did not try to construct a statue large enough to stand astride even the smallest of Rhodes's harbors, so that, as some Renaissance artists claimed, ships could sail between its legs. To do so, Helios would have been required to adopt

a grotesque stance with his feet 300 or 400 feet apart, a pose impossible even for Hellenistic ingenuity.

Placing the Colossus' legs close together presented Chares with more than enough technical challenges. After firmly anchoring the statue's feet and lower legs to a pedestal perhaps 40 feet high, he constructed a huge skeleton of stone pillars and iron bars. To this framework, carefully molded bronze plates were attached. For 12 years the statue grew piece by piece until a smooth bronze skin entirely covered the immense figure. When the surrounding mound of earth was removed and Helios stood for the citizens to see, Chares must have breathed a sigh of relief. He had effectively compensated for strong winds that would buffet his essentially fragile creation.

The statue was a brilliant advertisement for the city that built it, an awesome demonstration of affluence and technology. Unfortunately, time also proved it to be an example of extreme vulnerability. About 226 B.C., only 60-odd years after its inception, the Colossus crashed to earth, snapped at the knees by an earthquake.

Even after its calamitous fall, however, the statue ranked as a world-class wonder. Its shattered bronze body had already lain on the ground, like some Titan thrown down from heaven, for more than a hundred years when Antipater of Sidon, a Greco-Phoenician writer, included the Colossus in his list of Seven Wonders. As Pliny the Elder remarked in *Natural History*, "...even lying on the ground it is a marvel. Few people can make their arms meet round the thumb of the figure, and the fingers are larger than most statues; and where the limbs have broken off enormous cavities yawn, while inside are seen great masses of rock with the weight of which the artist steadied it when he erected it."

In A.D. 654, almost 900 years after the Colossus had collapsed, Arabs plundered Rhodes and sold Helios's remains for scrap. The buyer, a Jewish merchant from Asia Minor, reportedly used 900 camels to transport the fragments to their final destination in Syria. Ironically, the image of the deity who had once saved his city from invasion met a fate strangely reminiscent of Demetrius's infamous siege equipment, the sale of which had financed construction of the Colossus. Chares's giant statue was a wonder that, paradoxically, had illustrated both the glory and the vanity of human ambition.

Emblem of modern Rhodes, sculptures of deer gazing out to sea stand atop tall pillars flanking the entrance to Mandraki Harbor. Fort St. Nicolas, formerly considered the site of one of the Colossus's feet, rises in the background.

The Pharos of Alexandria

·········

Ancient Wonders

The Pharos of Alexandria towers above Egypt's flat, low coastline, its beacon guiding mariners to safe anchorage in the city's busy harbor.

As useful as it was conspicuous, the Pharos—lighthouse—of Alexandria towered an estimated 350 to 450 feet above the city's western harbor. The sole distinctive landmark on this low, featureless stretch of the Egyptian coast, it served to guide ships through a maze of submerged sandbars near the Nile Delta to the safety of Alexandria's protected docking area.

Named for the small, rocky island on which it stood, the Pharos was the only one of the Seven Wonders to have a practical function. By day, its polished metal mirrors (probably bronze) reflected sunlight far out to sea, alerting mariners to the secure passage it marked. By night, at least after the Roman occupation of Egypt, firelight was similarly projected. One celebrated Roman traveler, Pliny the Elder, was unimpressed by this innovation, however; he complained that from a distance the Pharos's beacon could easily be mistaken for a star hovering just above the horizon.

Because Greco-Roman craft rarely sailed after dark, the Pharos probably fulfilled its main purpose simply by its daytime high visibility. Almost as tall as the Great Pyramid, but with the vertical slimness of a modern skyscraper, the Pharos rose in three distinct stages. The first section, a square tower rising perhaps 235 feet above its base, stood on a stone platform that was about 360 feet square and 20 feet high. The interior of this stage resembled a vast, hollow, stone column; it was a cylindrical structure around which a ramp spiraled to the top, connecting the ground-floor entrance to the upper stories.

The second section, erected atop the first, was an octagon that may have been 115 feet high. A stairway led to the third stage, a cupola having a circular floor plan and measuring almost 30 feet across and 60 to 80 feet tall. Surmounting the entire edifice was a statue, probably of Zeus Soter, a flattering reference to the ruler who had begun this engineering marvel. Ptolemy I, a former general of Alexander the Great, had acquired Egypt after Alexander's death and assumed the title Soter—"Savior" (of his people). The actual costs of construction, however, were contributed by a rich diplomat or merchant, Sostratus of Cnidus. An inscription cited by the geographer Strabo records that Sostratus dedicated the Pharos "for the safety of those who sail the seas."

Completed early in the reign of Ptolemy's son, Ptolemy II (284-246 B.C.), the Pharos did more than help prevent shipwrecks and thus foster the economy of the Hellenistic world's busiest and wealthiest seaport. Its lofty spire of glistening white marble, rising higher than any other roofed building in the world, advertised the splendor of the city that Alexander, in 331 B.C., had marked out as the prototype of the Hellenistic metropolis. Named for its founder, Alexandria was carefully designed so that the long straight avenues of its grid plan were oriented to catch the cooling sea breezes. Alexander's city, positioned also to catch the flow of trade from three continents, grew with amazing rapidity. Its population eventually reached half a million, making it second only to Rome as the largest urban center of the late classical era.

With its back to Egypt's older cities, Alexandria faced the Mediterranean Sea, its merchants dispatching ships and sponsoring caravans that exchanged commercial goods from Ireland to India. Attracting wealth like a magnet, the port also drew investors, adventurers, philosophers, and con men—Greeks, Jews, Syrians, West Asians, and native Egyptians—who made Alexandria's citizenry one of antiquity's most ethnically and culturally diverse.

Lured by the prospect of royal patronage, many poets, painters, scientists, and scholars flocked to the capital, where Ptolemy I had established the

Founded by Alexander the Great in the fourth century B.C., Alexandria stood at the hub of a vast trading empire. A 1572 engraving shows the city as an Arab port after Egypt came under Islamic rule.

famous museum and library. Unlike modern museums that tend to display artifacts from the past, the Alexandria Museum was dedicated to the active service of the Muses, the nine daughters of Zeus who inspired artistic creativity. Functioning as a university, it sponsored both research and instruction; it was a Hellenistic think tank where, as one poet wrote, government-subsidized academics twittered endlessly "in the Muses's birdcage."

Ptolemaic kings were so eager to acquire books for Alexandria's library that one, Ptolemy III, ordered the seizure of all volumes carried by ships arriving in port. Copies were made and returned to their owners, but the originals were kept and labeled "from the ships." Wary of such royal rapacity, the Athenians insisted that Ptolemy pay a huge deposit before he could borrow the official transcripts of their three greatest playwrights: Aeschylus, Sophocles, and Euripides. Predictably, the king forfeited

his deposit and kept the plays, prize exhibits in a collection that eventually totaled about 490,000 volumes.

Besides preserving the literary heritage of archaic and classical Greece—most of what survives today we owe to Alexandrian scribes—the library also collected works of foreign origin. According to tradition, Ptolemy II commissioned copies of the Jewish Scriptures, and the result was the first translation of the Hebrew Bible into a modern tongue: the Greek Septuagint.

The most prominent symbol of Alexandria's opulence and technological expertise, the Pharos silently witnessed the decline of the classical civilization that had

Archaeologists attempting to reconstruct the appearance of the Pharos before it toppled must rely on ancient travelers' descriptions and images on coins. The coin above shows the lighthouse's three distinct stages.

Submerged since the Pharos collapsed into the sea in the 14th century, a pink granite bust (left) that once adorned the 350-to-450-foot lighthouse emerges from the Mediterranean Sea in October 1995.

given it birth. In A.D. 476, the western Roman Empire collapsed after being overrun by Gothic hordes. Although the eastern (Byzantine) part of the empire survived, it could not protect Egypt from invasion by Persian armies early in the seventh century. Far more decisive was the Arab conquest in A.D. 642, which permanently transformed polyglot Alexandria into an Islamic city.

After earthquakes had damaged the lighthouse's lantern, an Egyptian caliph erected a small mosque at the top. The edifice was still largely intact when a Moslem traveler from Spain, el-Badawi el-Andalusi, visited it in 1166 and described its main structural features. In 1326, another Moslem observer, Abu Abd Allah Mohammed Ibn Battuta, also found most of the Pharos still standing: "I went to see the lighthouse on this occasion and found one of its faces in ruins [probably from the severe earthquakes of 946 and 1303]. It is a very high square building, and its door is above the level of the earth.... Inside the door is a place for the lighthouse keeper, and within the lighthouse there are many chambers."

Returning in 1349, Ibn Battuta discovered that the Pharos's condition had significantly deteriorated: "It had fallen into so ruinous a condition that it was not possible to enter it or climb up to the door."

Egyptian records state that a major quake in 1375 toppled most of the remaining walls, more than 1,650 years after they were first constructed. Demolition of the once

Pompey's Pillar, a 72-foot-tall granite column, stands as Alexandria's most prominent antiquity (above). Misnamed by European travelers, it honors a Roman emperor. Nearby rests a Ptolemaic granite sphinx recalling ancient Alexandria's international nature.

Built on the Pharos's foundation, Qait Bey Fortress (right) still commands a harbor where archaeologists recently discovered statuary and stonework that fell from the Pharos more than 600 years ago.

proud tower was completed in 1480 when Mameluke Sultan Qait Bey used its stones to build a large fortress on the site, a harbor defense that stands in the bay.

Underwater exploration of Alexandria's harbor has recently recovered some sculptures and finely cut stone that may once have decorated the Pharos. Except for these fragments, little remains to mark the place where Hellenistic architects—determined to help vulnerable mariners avoid nature's trap—erected one of the highest masonry structures ever built.

The medieval mind, like the classical mind before it, was captivated by the wondrous things people had made—perhaps even more so. For much of the thousand-year period known as the Middle Ages, most Europeans lived in small, isolated communities; travel was difficult and often dangerous; and knowledge was confined to, and often controlled by, men of the church. The great civilizations of Greece and Rome were long gone, but even so, some of their glory was still remembered. And tales of an incredible civilization in the East, brought back by intrepid travelers, had begun to excite the European imagination.

Following the third century B.C., when the earliest known list of wonders was compiled, successive scholars and philosophers modified and updated the list of ancient wonders to reflect their own opinions. At some point, during or maybe after the Middle Ages, another list appeared—the medieval world's Seven Wonders.

The surviving list of medieval wonders holds a particular fascination because only some of its marvels actually date from the Middle Ages. This list also includes even older structures that, in the medieval mind, were considered great accomplishments. Imaginative and eclectic, the list represents almost 4,500 years of human endeavor. England's Stonehenge, Rome's Colosseum, and Constantinople's Hagia Sophia are miracles of monumentality, while the Porcelain Tower of Nanjing and the Leaning Tower of Pisa have an almost whimsical fascination. Alexandria's Catacombs of Kom el Shoqafa and China's Great Wall stand as symbols of cultural endurance.

Surprisingly, only one of the great churches erected by medieval builders—Hagia Sophia— made the list. But perhaps it simply takes time and centuries of human admiration to acquire that distinctive patina of wonder.

SEVEN WONDERS of the MEDIEVAL MIND

....

by K. M. Kostyal

Defying time and terrain, the centuries-old, 3,000-mile-long Great Wall still stands—a symbol of China's history and perseverance.

Stonehenge

··········

Medieval Wonders

Massive sarsens mark Stonehenge's
outer circle. Medieval scholars declared
this ring of multiton megaliths, hauled
into place about 4,000 years ago, a
"wonder of England."

or 4,000 years, Stonehenge has stood on the windswept downs of southern England and haunted the human imagination. A ring of massive, unfathomable stones, it is not so much a structure as it is a creation in stone: Its precise creators remain unknown, its purpose ultimately is unknowable, and the very fact of its existence is a marvel.

How did Neolithic and Bronze Age peoples, struggling to survive as simple farmers, move megaliths hundreds of miles and then raise them into upright configurations of concentric circles and horseshoes? And why did they bother? What is the significance of the site and its separate parts? Stonehenge is much more than the stones themselves.

This megalithic wonder did not take shape in just a few years or decades. In fact, several centuries went by. Over the course of 1,600 years, the look and the builders of Stonehenge changed. The original construction was spare, not the impressive stand of megaliths we think of today. The first signs of it appeared on the chalky downs of present-day Wiltshire about 2950 B.C., when Neolithic builders began scratching a circular ditch into the earth with picks made from deer antlers. They piled the dirt from the ditch into a six-foot-high bank, eventually enclosing a space about 330 feet across.

Within the dirt bank, the builders dug 56 small holes now called Aubrey Holes. Archaeologists were baffled by their purpose for years, but they now believe the holes held wooden posts. In time the wood decayed and left deep indentations in a circular pattern. At some point between 2900 and 2400 B.C., several of the holes became repositories for cremated human bones.

Wooden uprights also appear to have been positioned inside the enclosure. For more than 500 years, Stonehenge was apparently only a large earthen enclosure with timber settings. Then other builders began to reconfigure it, moving its axis to the east and cutting an "avenue" that was oriented with remarkable accuracy to the rising of the sun at the midsummer solstice. A double circle of bluestones started to rise in the interior, but for some reason, the circle was never completed; the stones, hauled to the site from the Preseli Mountains of western Wales, were removed. Soon after this, the great sarsens—a form of very hard sandstone—made their appearance. Ten honed megaliths, from the Marlborough Downs 25 miles away, were placed in a horseshoe arrangement at the

Marvel in the making: Stonehenge evolved over about 1,600 years. It began as a circular earthen embankment (top) surrounding a ring of wooden posts and perhaps a central timber structure. A thousand years later, new builders erected a monumental circle of linked sarsen stones and raised an inner horseshoe of trilithons (middle). In the next millennium, a circle and horseshoe of smaller bluestones completed the site (bottom).

A fanciful aquatint (below) perpetuates the long-standing myth that Druids erected Stonehenge as a ceremonial site. No such revelries disturb the stones today: A rope barrier keeps visitors at a respectful distance (opposite) .

slowly-evolving ceremonial precinct."

Over the next thousand years, smaller bluestones were added. Their configurations were changed until at last the stones formed a horseshoe inside the sarsen horseshoe, as well as an outer bluestone circle between the two sarsen configurations. The so-called Altar Stone was placed within the horseshoe and that, apparently, ended construction.

All the work since that time has been deconstruction—both physically and symbolically. Over eons, weather has toppled some stones, and man has marauded others, "quarrying" them for roads and other building projects. In the 18th century, souvenir hunters came armed with hammers to chip away at the megaliths and take home pieces of Stonehenge. Happily, though, the stones were "so exceeding hard," according to one such hunter, "that all my strength with a hammer, could not breake a fragment."

center of the enclosure. Huge lintels were laid atop each pair, forming five trilithons, or squared arches. Around them was placed a ring of slightly smaller sarsens rising about 13.5 feet from the ground and bearing their own lintels. The ends of each lintel were carved with grooves that attached to their neighbors. "The stone circle," writes scholar Rodney Castleden, "is neither the oldest nor the largest part of the monument: it is the final embellishment—a kind of summary—at the centre of a large and

Scientists, theorists, cultists, and quacks have been searching out Stonehenge's meaning and origins for centuries. Historian Geoffrey of Monmouth was the first to tackle the problem in his *History of the Kings of Britain,* written about 1136. Confidently, he explained that Stonehenge was a monument erected to 460 British chieftains massacred by the treacherous Saxons. The British king Aurelius Ambrosius had authorized the memorial, and the wizard Merlin suggested to him that stones from the Giants' Round on Ireland's Mount Killaraus would make an appropriate monument. But the strength of mere mortals could not budge the blocks of giants, and it took Merlin's magic to "sette the stones there that the kynge wold bane hem.... When the kyng sawe that it was made he thanked Merlyn and richely him rewarded at his own wylle & that place lete calle Stonhenge for evermore."

Monmouth's legend lasted hundreds of years. Then, suddenly, Druids, Danes, Romans, Greeks, and Egyptians alternately were given builder's credit. Using radiocarbon dating, modern scientists have at last been able to place Stonehenge in the Neolithic period and the succeeding Bronze Age, far before most of these purported builders.

As the winter sun shines through a gap in the megaliths, its rays just miss the outer Heel Stone (above). To some scholars, the stones' alignment suggests that Stonehenge functioned as an astronomical calendar. Using simple stone tools, sculptors likely worked years to shape each megalith (opposite). In time, weathering added its own embellishments.

In 1965, astronomer Gerald Hawkins declared, almost as confidently as Geoffrey of Monmouth, that he knew the purpose of the megaliths. After feeding data into an IBM computer, Hawkins became convinced that Stonehenge had been a gigantic "neolithic computer," designed to predict and follow movements of the sun and moon.

The observatory theory still has adherents; so does the Druidic theory. Endlessly attracted to Stonehenge, New Age Druids and assorted cultists flock to the site even though a rope barrier now keeps them 50 feet away. Whatever its original purpose may have been, this much can be asserted: Stonehenge has become, as one writer puts it, "*the* Temple of the nation. Not a ruin, or monument of lost traditions, but a living Temple still in use."

The Colosseum

....

Medieval Wonders

"Stupendous, yet beautiful in its
destruction," wrote painter Thomas
Cole of Rome's most famous ruin.
For 18 centuries it ranked as the
world's largest coliseum.

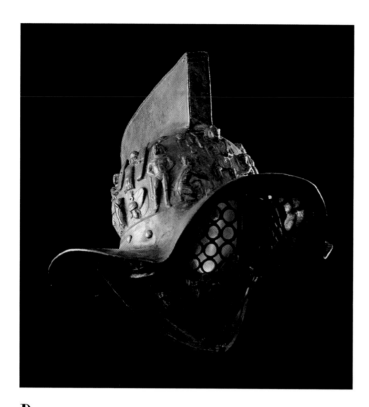

Rome suffered under the emperor Nero for 14 years, until at last he took his own life in A.D. 68. A year later the judicious Vespasian, one of Nero's former commanders, ascended the throne and returned stability and reason to the land. In a gesture clearly designed to please Rome's citizens, he ordered that a new amphitheater be built to replace one damaged in a fire that had swept the city under Nero. The colossal structure would stand on the site of an artificial lake in Nero's former pleasure garden. This site was symbolic: "Rome has been restored to herself...," declared the poet Martial. "That is now the delight of the people which was formerly a tyrant's."

The people's delight was understandable, for the august amphitheater was unprecedented in size. It took ten years and three emperors—Titus Flavius Vespasianus, better known as Vespasian, and his two sons—to complete the Flavian Amphitheater, as it came to be called. But the time spent was negligible if considered historically, because for 18 centuries the structure would stand as the largest amphitheater ever built.

An ellipse measuring 615 by 510 feet, the amphitheater rose to a height of 159 feet and could hold about 50,000 spectators. Resting on a foundation 40 feet deep, its infrastructure was brick, concrete, and tufa, while the

A gladiator's ceremonial helmet (left) conjures grisly images of the blood sport that enthralled Colosseum audiences for more than 300 years.

Now floorless, greened with grass, and reduced to a third of its original size, the Colosseum (above) endures as a symbol of Eternal Rome.

exterior was faced in blocks of travertine limestone. The 80 entrance arches ringing the ground level were flanked

horsemen; above them sat distinguished citizens, then the middle class. Another level was reserved for slaves and foreigners, and, finally, high at the top, seats were allocated for women and the poor. Though open to the sky, the structure could be covered by a *velarium,* a huge awning unfurled by the emperor's sailors to protect crowds from the sun or rain.

Weaned on class status and cruelty, the Romans were a rapacious audience, both as spectators and as an electorate. They expected their emperor to feed them and to entertain them—preferably with gory spectacles. The Colosseum provided a massive venue for satisfying the Roman appetite. Even before the structure was completed, the emperor staged inaugural games in it that lasted a hundred days. Neither sporting nor lighthearted, these gladiatorial contests were deadly encounters between men and men, and men and beasts. The festivities took the lives of "five thousand beasts of different sorts...in a single day."

From sunrise until after nightfall, the gladiators performed in the massive arena, whose wooden floor was covered with the sand *(arena)* that gave the performance area its name and which soaked up

by engaged Doric columns. Arched bays may have held statuary ornamenting the second and third levels, whose flanking columns respectively displayed Ionic and Corinthian architectural motifs. Topping all this, the attic level was enclosed by a wall having Corinthian pilasters.

The seating within these multitiers perfectly reflected Roman class and social status. At the level closest to the arena, a lavish podium held the marble seats reserved for the emperor and his guests; next came senators and

the blood spilled in the sport. The arena could even be outfitted with exotic jungles that would serve as backdrops for contests pitting men against wild animals.

Below the arena's wooden floor, a warren of small chambers and corridors was crowded with stagehands who ensured that the mechanics of the performances went well. In that sweltering, belowground space, animals paced in their cages and the gladiators waited their turns to perform, perhaps to die. Most were convicted

criminals or prisoners of war chosen for gladiatorial training, possibly because they were thought to have talent for savagery. Their barracks, the Ludus Magnus, lay nearby. Though hardly free men, the successful among them nonetheless became popular heroes, particularly among the female population. But gladiators were not the only figures to appear in the arena. As the centuries progressed, great numbers of Christians were martyred on the sands of the Colosseum. Reviled by the Roman populace, these new religious zealots were rumored to practice incest, cannibalism, and other heinous acts. Such rumors gave the rulers reason to kill the Christian "revolutionaries." Some were burned alive, while others were shot by arrows or thrown to the lions.

The persecutions came to an end during the reign of Emperor Constantine, who in A.D. 312 turned Rome toward Christianity. When the emperor shifted his seat of power to Constantinople, in the east, Rome settled into a slow decline, and in 404, the last gladiatorial games were held in the great Colosseum. A few years later, Visigoths entered Rome and sacked the city. As the centuries wore on, conquering armies time and again descended on the Eternal City, but they did little damage to the Colosseum. What did devour its massive walls were periodic earthquakes and the quarrying of its stone for new Roman buildings, which finally reduced the structure to a state of semiruin. And yet the Colosseum was still too imposing an achievement to be ignored.

In the Middle Ages, powerful feudal families commandeered the mighty ruin, using it as a fortress, and the church later used it for housing and workshops. Eventually, a massive earthquake collapsed the southwest facade, and the structure fell into desuetude. For almost four centuries, it served the purpose of a quarry. Local builders could come and help themselves to fine travertine blocks that once had adorned the greatest amphitheater in the world.

In 1744, the destruction ended when a papal edict dedicated the site to martyrs who had fallen there. By then European Romantics had discovered the half-walled, floorless splendor of the Colosseum and were writing about its pathos and immensity. Even with only a third of its original form intact, the monument somehow had not been diminished. "When one looks at it," the German poet Goethe wrote, "all else seems little; the edifice is so vast, that one cannot hold the image of it in one's soul...."

Streaking lights of modern rush hour circle the ancient structure in this time exposure. Its intact northeast facade still rises the original 159 feet.

The Catacombs of Kom el Shoqafa

Medieval Wonders

Carved from subterranean rock,
Alexandria's haunting, 1,900-year-old
necropolis celebrates a blending of
artistic motifs from Egyptian and
Greco-Roman traditions.

Alexandria, Egypt, represented a melding of cultures in the late first century A.D. Traditions of Greece and Rome overlay the city, the cult of Christianity was gaining ground, and memories of ancient Egypt's great kingdoms still lingered. It was a place where people seemed to have a talent for combining rather than destroying cultures.

Little of that "Paris of antiquity" has survived above the ground. Below it, however, are haunting reminders of a culture that existed 1,900 years ago: the Catacombs of Kom el Shoqafa, "Mound of Shards." Carved out of solid rock, three levels burrow into ground near the sites of the ancient stadium and the long-vanished temple to Serapis, a Greek and Egyptian god. Many such catacombs once filigreed Alexandria's underground, but earthquakes and

construction projects destroyed or obscured them. Only in 1900 was Kom el Shoqafa rediscovered after centuries —by a donkey that fell through a hole in the ground and into its access well. The animal, it soon became clear, had made an extraordinary archaeological find.

An ancient circular staircase leads down into the catacombs. In the late second century, when Kom el Shoqafa was an active burial site, bodies were lowered by rope down the well formed by the spiraling stairs. The staircase ends at a landing vestibule, where two benches are carved into wall niches overarched by the cockleshell motif often found in classical designs.

A rotunda pierced by a six-pillared central shaft opens off the vestibule. To the left lies the *triclinium,* the funeral

banquet hall where friends and family gathered on stone couches covered with cushions. Here they reclined while ceremonially feasting in memory of the deceased. Scholars believe that the catacombs at first may have served one family, but they were expanded into a mass burial site, probably administered by a corporation with dues-paying members. This theory could explain why so many chambers were hewn from the rock.

A staircase from the rotunda descends to the second level, an area eerily alive with sculpture (the third level is flooded and inaccessible). In the vestibule, two pillars are topped by the papyrus, lotus, and acanthus leaves of ancient Egypt, their frieze adorned by two falcons flanking a winged sun. Carved into wall niches are figures of a man and a woman, perhaps the tomb's original occupants. The man's body assumes the stiff hieratic pose found in ancient Egyptian sculpture, but his head is in the lifelike manner of the classical Hellenes; the woman's stance is also rigid, but she sports a Roman hairstyle. Overseeing the adjoining burial chamber are two sculptures of the Egyptian dog-headed god, Anubis. But one has a crocodile tail, suggesting the god Sobek. Both bear the armor of a Roman soldier. "Perhaps the queer couple were meant to guard the tomb," quipped writer E. M. Forster, "but one must not read too much into them or into anything here; the workmen employed were only concerned to turn out a room that should look suitable for death, and judged by this standard they have succeeded." Continuing this motif, if it can be called that, bas-relief serpents on the walls wear the double crown of Upper and Lower Egypt and bear the staff of Hermes and the pinecone of Dionysus.

Three gigantic sarcophagi with lids that do not lift rest along the sides of the chamber. Scholars assume that bodies would have been inserted into them from behind, using a passageway that runs around the outside of the funeral chamber. The unusual way in which the traditional Egyptian deities are depicted in this chamber led archaeologist Gaston Maspero to write: "If we remember the degree of popularity enjoyed by Isis throughout the Roman Empire, there is nothing to stop us supposing that this Egyptian décor housed the remains of a foreigner in some way associated with the worship of that goddess...." Further circling this central tomb chamber is a hallway

Behind the principal sarcophagus, a relief (left) depicts the dog-headed Egyptian god, Anubis, and his attendants ministering to Osiris's mummified body.

Rigidly posed but with realistically modeled features, this statue (above) may represent a likeness of one of the tomb's original occupants.

with 91 wall niches, each one providing burial space for three mummies.

Returning to the first level, visitors can reach a separate set of tombs through a breach in the rotunda wall, unintended by the original builders. It leads to what has been called the Hall of Caracalla, where bones of horses and humans were found. The hall's name comes from an episode in A.D. 215, when Emperor Caracalla ordered Alexandrian youths to a review, then massacred them.

As much as its cavernous size and ornamentation, it is the hybridization of design found in the Catacombs of Kom el Shoqafa that inspires wonder. "Any visitor is likely to be more impressed by it than by anything else he sees in Alexandria," writes one scholar. It is "visible evidence of an age when three cultures, three arts and three religions were superimposed upon Egyptian soil."

The Great Wall

··········

Medieval Wonders

Form and function combine in the sinuous grace of the Great Wall. Towers, fortresses, castles, and even temples punctuate the complex barricade across northern China.

So immense a feat of engineering is China's Great Wall that its length is still being determined. For about 3,000 miles, according to the latest estimate, it snakes across the northern part of the country "like some great sleeping dragon, stretching and sunning itself on the peaks and ridges of some of the most beautiful mountain scenery in the world."

As legendary as the Chinese dragon, the Great Wall is also just as chimerical as that phantasmagoric beast. The wall has become a symbol of national pride and ancient greatness—a single grand structure that stretches from Jiayuguan, near the northwestern desert, to Shanhaiguan, near the Yellow Sea.

Historians and legend makers long believed that the origins of the Great Wall could be traced to the First Emperor, Qin Shihuang, who unified the Warring States late in the third century B.C. He is said to have decreed

Intricate embellishments on the Great Wall's Cloud Terrace Gate in Beijing (left) betoken China's long civilization and love of art.

Near Hohhot, a desert trail (above) follows the route of one of the earliest walls across north China. Built in the fourth century B.C., the wall tumbled long ago.

that a vast fortification be built to keep out the nomadic hordes threatening his lands from their own homelands in the Mongolian steppes. These mobile, horse-borne peoples moved with the seasons, following their flocks

Buttressing the western edge of empire, the Great Wall's gate at Jiayuguan Pass once oversaw Silk Road caravans carrying the treasures of China—silk, jade, tea, spices, and gold—across the deserts of Central Asia to ports along the Mediterranean Sea.

and recognizing no political borders. The Chinese themselves had few horses and no reliable army with which to combat the swift, fierce tribesmen. A stationary fortification seemed the reasonable solution—a long wall.

Preceding rulers in the area had constructed less ambitious walls to protect their territories, and historians now believe that Qin's wall linked existing walls into one unified line of defense. The project must have taken an enormous number of civilian hands and tens of thousands of soldiers to achieve. But today very little evidence of the Qin wall remains to give credence to the myth of its vastness or provide a clue to its exact location.

In the centuries that followed, nomads continued to threaten and rulers, both imperial and local, continued to sporadically build walls to keep them out. No doubt the legendary Qin wall was also maintained and restored as part of this process. But the true Great Wall began to take shape almost 15 centuries after the emperor Qin's demise, during the Ming Dynasty (1368-1644).

In the first decades of the Ming reign, no wall seems to have separated the Ming from the Mongols, and in

1449, Mongols dealt the Ming army a stunning blow at a place called T'u-mu. A quarter of a century later, in 1474, the Chinese made a strategic decision to build a defense south of the Ordos, a desert area lying within the great loop of the Yellow River where they hoped they could contain the Mongols. From behind their defensive buffer, the Ming would be able to cultivate the land to support a military presence. A large wall would have to be built to hold the Mongols back, however. And so the Great Wall was begun.

Like previous walls, this structure undoubtedly included parts of existing ones. Initially, the new sections were made of earth, but as Ming builders extended the wall over the next century, they increasingly used stone. After leveling the ground, they laid a foundation of stone

slabs averaging 25 feet in width. From this, two outer walls of stone and brick rose 20 to 30 feet and sloped inward to create what is called a battered wall. The area between these two walls was filled with smaller stones, rubble, and earth. A wide path, typically about 15 feet across, ran along the top of the wall, allowing troops and messengers to move with ease through the terrain.

Turn-of-the-century visitors contemplate the Great Wall and its environs (above). Partially destroyed during the Cultural Revolution instituted by Mao Tse-tung in the 1960s, the wall has since regained its stature as a pilgrimage site. Today, travelers from many parts of the world, as well as the people of China, flock to the Great Wall, paying homage to the greatest fortification ever built (opposite).

In the course of its 3,000 miles, however, the Great Wall was far more than just a wall. It was punctuated, generally every 11 miles, by beacon towers that used smoke or fire to signal warnings of impending attack. But these towers were just one aspect of the wall. In all, some 25,000 gates, watchtowers, castles, fortresses, and guardhouses—even an occasional temple and shrine—were built into the structure of the wall.

For all its grandeur, the Great Wall was not always a successful barrier. Aggressors periodically penetrated far into the Chinese interior despite its presence. In 1550, Altan Khan simply went around a section of the wall to make his attack. The Mings survived that debacle, but they could not survive the formidable Manchus, who occupied territory on the northeastern frontier. In 1644, the Manchus stormed Beijing, bringing an end to the nearly 300-year-long rule of the Ming Dynasty. Their wall, however, survived them, and through the centuries it became a legend. Stories of its grandeur were carried back to Europe and spread throughout the world by explorers and merchants who had seen it. In China, myths sprang up that centered on the Great Wall, and in the West, it was proclaimed to be one of the greatest of human achievements.

Although time and the ravages of war gradually collapsed or weakened parts of the Great Wall, the structure continued to be a symbol of China. Even Mao Tse-tung, the leader of the Communist Revolution, wrote two known poems about it, one of which read:

Either side of the Great Wall
One blinding vastness....
To touch this pure white with a blush of rose—
O, enchantment past compare!

But Mao and his minions later turned against all vestiges of China's ancient glory. During the devastating Cultural Revolution, the wall was attacked and long stretches of it were dismantled for building projects. When the destruction at last abated, China looked at her Great Wall with new eyes. In 1984, Communist leader Deng Xiaoping reversed Mao, declaring, "Let us love our country and restore our Great Wall." And so once again the Chinese have turned to restoring their wall, which, like their civilization, has seen centuries of turmoil mixed with progress, yet continues to endure.

Pagoda-roofed Western Tower at Jiayuguan Pass originally marked the boundary between the civilized world of 14th-century Ming emperors and the untempered wilds of Central Asia.

The Porcelain Tower of Nanjing

Medieval Wonders

· · · · · · · · · ·

Centerpiece of the Baoen Monastery outside Nanjing, the Porcelain Tower quickly became an emblem of sublime engineering, as much admired by Europeans as by Buddhist worshipers.

The people of China called it *Bao'ensi,* the "Temple of Gratitude." European visitors who beheld the structure called it the Porcelain Tower of Nanjing and labeled it one of the wonders of the world. But warfare and subsequent destruction overtook it in the 19th century, and this remarkable structure was almost lost to history, virtually forgotten by the world.

Still, for the many people who had known the tower firsthand, it was a sublimely elegant example of a Buddhist pagoda. "The best contrived and noblest structure of all the east," wrote Le Comte, the French mathematician who had made a visit to China in the early 19th century.

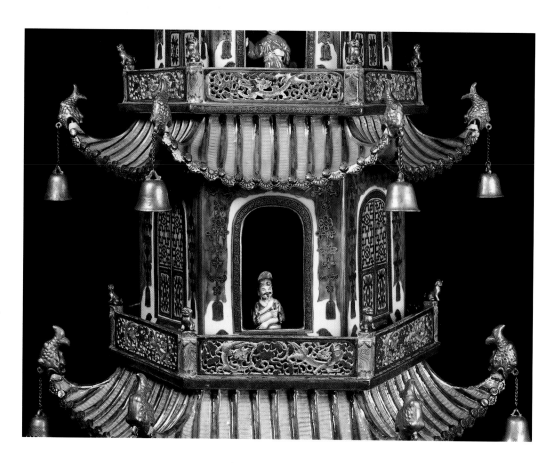

Miniaturized for posterity, a nine-foot porcelain pagoda in London's Victoria and Albert Museum (opposite) may depict Nanjing's nine-story tower. The figurine's elaborate detailing (above) captures the finesse of such pagoda temples.

From an octagonal base about 97 feet in diameter, the tower's nine stories rose pyramidally to a height of about 260 feet. According to information obtained by an American missionary who journeyed to Nanjing in 1852, the original plan for the tower had called for 13 stories and a total height of about 330 feet. Although those ambitious dimensions were never realized, the smaller size made little difference, because size was not what made the structure so memorable for visitors.

The brilliant white porcelain bricks that faced the tower were what made it so unforgettable. By day, the bricks glittered in the sun, and at night they were illuminated by perhaps as many as 140 lamps hanging around the exterior of the pagoda. Worked into the porcelain panels were colorful stoneware tiles with green, yellow, white, and brown glazes forming images of animals, landscapes, flowers, and bamboo.

The upward sloping roofs that capped each of the tower's progressively narrower nine stories were covered by green tiles and hung with bells. One visitor reported that a total of 152 bells could be heard tinkling in the breeze. Woodwork that was "strong, curiously carved, and richly painted" supported the roofs. From the eighth story a tall pole extended up through the final floor and became a spire above the gold-encrusted roof of the building. Spiraling round the spire itself was an iron ring topped by a flame-shaped ball.

Awed visitors and the devout Buddhists who entered this temple found themselves standing inside an octagonal pavilion that was lighted by 12 oil-burning porcelain lamps. The light shone upward, touching the floors above. It was said to have illuminated the "thirty-three heavens" and brought "to light the good and evil among men, for ever banishing human evils." A spiral staircase containing 190 steps ascended through the floors of the temple, and on each of these floors could be found niches holding Buddhist statuary. On the very top level of the structure, observers would stand and catch their breath as long views across the city of Nanjing spread out in all directions.

Nanjing itself, the city laid out on the banks of the Yangtze, had been the "southern capital" for only a few

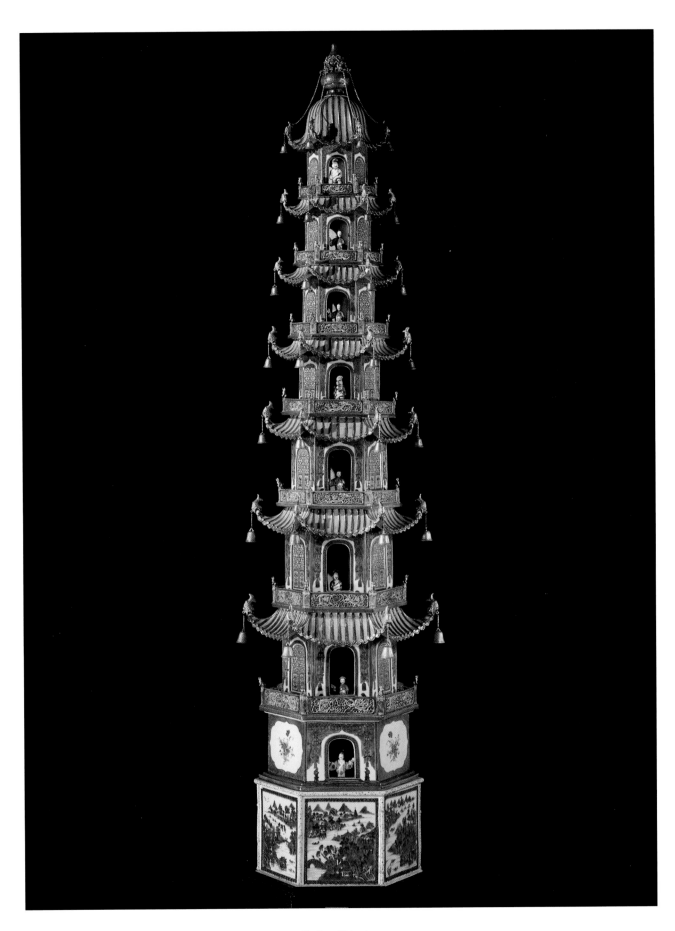

decades when the Ming Dynasty's Yongle emperor, in the early 15th century, issued the command authorizing construction of the temple. The new temple would rise to replace an earlier tower that had stood in the Baoen Monastery complex on the outskirts of the city. According to a legend purporting to explain the emperor's purpose, the Porcelain Tower was built to honor "the virtues of his deceased august empress mother." But after much research, some scholars have now come to believe that the magnificent tower instead was meant to be a loving

tribute by the emperor to both of his deceased parents. In either case, what is known by researchers who have studied the written record is that workers took almost seven years to complete the temple. By that time, Yongle had left Nanjing behind and relocated to the northern capital at Beijing. But the tower suffered no diminution in size or respect as a result of the emperor's desertion, and it soon became recognized as a hallmark of the city. Visitors would refer in one breath to Nanjing and its remarkable Porcelain Tower.

Legends of the Porcelain Tower's delicate allure survive in both art and literature. In a 1790 European engraving (left), the pagoda rises before distant, swirling hills.

Its "many-coloured tiles and bricks were highly glazed, giving the building a gay and beautiful appearance," recalled a 19th-century American missionary. Probably a rare remnant of the tower facade, the elegant elephant tile above measures 9 inches by 13 inches.

Such structures often were built to attract the attention of the local gods and to bring their blessings down to the grateful populace. For almost four hundred years, the Porcelain Tower of Nanjing apparently succeeded in its mission—until the 19th century. Things started to change for the worse in 1801. During a storm, a bolt of lightning destroyed the tower's top three stories, but they were rebuilt not long after. Then, in 1853, the Taiping Rebels, who were led by a Christian zealot pronouncing himself to be the younger brother of Jesus Christ, took control of

Nanjing and established their capital at the city. Sometime between 1853 and 1864, the rebels blew up the Buddhists' famous Porcelain pagoda and carried off most of its bricks. They apparently feared that the geomantic power of the tower could still hurt their cause. When Imperial forces finally were able to oust the Taipings in 1865, the city lay in ruins and there was no talk of rebuilding its notable tower.

One of the wonders of the world had been destroyed by warfare and religious strife, and very little of the once lovely tower remained for contemplation. Fortunately, memories of its much-admired design were not completely lost. Fascinated by pagodas as symbols of the exotic East, Europeans in the 17th, 18th, and 19th centuries frequently copied them. Some scholars believe that the landmark pagoda rising in London's venerable Kew Gardens was inspired by Nanjing's famous tower.

In the heyday of Chinese export goods, Europeans also had a penchant for miniature pagodas replicated in exquisite detail. A particularly serene example in the collection of London's Victoria and Albert Museum has a handwritten note at its base: "by the Emperor Yung Lo.... Its name in Chinese was...the Pagoda of Gratitude."

The Hagia Sophia

....

Medieval Wonders

Nearly 1,500 years of history shaped
Hagia Sophia, triumph of Istanbul. Over-
looking the Bosporus, it once served as
Christendom's greatest basilica and as
an eminent Ottoman mosque.

For centuries it stood at the heart of two of the world's great religions: To Christians it was Hagia Sophia, Church of the Holy Wisdom, mother church of the Orthodox faith and of the thousand-year-old Byzantine Empire. To Muslims, it became Ayasofya Camii, Mosque of Holy Wisdom and jewel of Istanbul. But to people of all faiths, it was, in the words of sixth-century historian Procopius, a "spectacle of marvellous beauty, overwhelming to those who see it, but to those who know it by hearsay altogether incredible. For it soars to a height to match the sky...stands on high and looks down on the remainder of the city...."

In A.D. 326, Constantinople was laid out on the shores of the Bosporus by Emperor Constantine. Thirty years later, his successor built its first great church—eventually called Hagia Sophia—but it stood only 172 years before rioting crowds burned it to the ground. This event, in 532, was perhaps auspicious: It occurred during the reign of Justinian the Builder, who would give the world the sublime "tent of the heavens" that still stands and in whose creation "God has surely taken part."

Though long ago stripped of its Byzantine adornments, Hagia Sophia's interior still resonates with an ethereal swirl of light and immensity (opposite).

In one of Hagia Sophia's few surviving mosaics (above), Emperors Justinian, at left, and Constantine, at right, attend the Madonna and Child.

Justinian's Hagia Sophia rose on the foundations of the former church, but its design was different from the familiar cruciform shape of Western churches. Instead of appointing architects to the task of bringing his dream to fruition, Justinian selected two Greeks from Asia Minor: a theoretician and geometer named Anthemius and a natural scientist named Isidorus.

Construction began just 39 days after the destruction of the original church. To oversee the work himself, Justinian had an imperial "retiring room" built on-site. And in order to hasten construction, he split 10,000 laborers and foremen into two competing groups, one working on the right half, the other on the left half of the structure.

The gigantic structure was modeled loosely on the Roman Pantheon. Measuring 220 feet by 250 feet along its main floor, it was laid out as a rectangle, at whose center was a square. Soaring 180 feet above the square was a dome supported by four massive pendentives on equally massive piers. At the east and west ends of the dome square—and pressing in on it to lend structural support—were two half domes serving as the apse and entrance bay. These were supported by two smaller half domes, so that at each end a triad of half domes flanked the central dome on the east-west axis. North and south of the central square, barrel vaults helped support the sides of the church. The engineering feat was even more incredible considering that only brick, mortar, and stone were used. Although the earlier Romans knew how to make concrete, these Eastern builders did not.

Justinian embellished the interior with riches. Four acres of gold mosaics shimmered from the ceiling, and multicolored marble gleamed from floors, columns, and wall panels, their polished surfaces catching the light

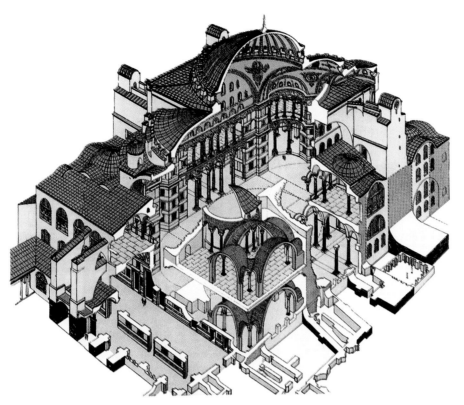

Sixth-century builders stretched the limits of their art to construct the massive central dome (above). Ribs, piers, and arches help support it; semidomes and half domes brace its east-west axis.

Inspired by Hagia Sophia, Islamic architects designed domed buildings throughout the city. To the basilica (left), they added the minarets of a mosque.

from the thousands of lamps and candelabra that illuminated every level. Silk hangings dangled above the altar, and a marble atrium served as an entryway.

Less than six years after work on it began, Justinian's monument to Christendom was completed. But it quickly became more than a building in stone, evolving and changing its physical aspect as times changed—and as its structure succumbed to defects in design. The dome proved a recurrent problem in the earthquake-prone area along the Bosporus, and in A.D. 558 much of it collapsed. Because the initial architects, Anthemius and Isidorus, were no longer living, the latter's nephew, Isidorus the Younger, was given the task of rebuilding. His new dome rose 20 feet higher, displacing its weight more easily along the supports and surviving 400 years before it, too,

collapsed and had to be rebuilt.

During those 400 years, other changes were wrought within the Church of the Holy Wisdom. Elaborate mosaics of saints and other human figures were put up, then pulled down by Iconoclasts within the church, then executed yet again as theologies and factions within the faith changed. But factionalism at last led to a permanent split in Christendom, dividing it into the Orthodox East and the Roman Catholic West. In 1204, knights of the Fourth Crusade marched on the Byzantine Empire's capital city, stripping it and Hagia Sophia so remorselessly that a chronicler called it the most awesome plunder "since the creation of the world."

When Rome's hegemony ended 57 years later, the Church of the Holy Wisdom was devoid of glittering wealth. Bulky buttresses were built to shore it up, but its days of glory, and those of Constantinople, were drawing to a close. In 1453, Sultan Mohammed II massed the Ottoman army in front of the city. After a 53-day siege, the Byzantine Empire's great capital capitulated, and the conqueror marched into town and directly to Hagia Sophia. His *ulama* recited a Muslim prayer, and the sultan declared Eastern Christianity's cornerstone a mosque.

For almost 500 years it remained such, its mosaics whitewashed to hide the "idolatrous" figures of humans. Koranic inscriptions were placed in the four corners beneath the dome; four minarets were erected at the corners of the exterior perimeter; a gilded bronze crescent replaced the large metal cross crowning the basilica.

While the changes offended Christians, the Mosque of Holy Wisdom enjoyed a place of high regard among devotees of Islam. In the 20th century, Turkish leader Kemal Atatürk viewed the structure as a unifying symbol for East and West. He closed the mosque in 1932, uncovered its medieval mosaics, and reopened Hagia Sophia as a museum in 1934. Nearly 15 centuries after Justinian, it stands as a monument to both human and divine wisdom.

Medieval Wonders
....

pronounced. Again the Pisans brought everything to a halt, pausing for almost a century. Finally, in 1350, the still leaning tower was finished.

Its unfortunate feature did not make it unique, however. Other European towers of that era leaned as well. But the angle of Pisa's Leaning Tower became more and more remarkable as the campanile literally began to screw itself into the soft ground, leaning at first to the northwest, then to the north, to the east, and to the south, where it still slants today. Despite its instability, or perhaps because of it, the tower has risen into the ranks of world-class landmarks.

Today, no resident of Pisa would willingly part with such a distinction by having the famous tower righted. And besides, no one seems to know how to fix the problem. But the worrisome situation, if not at least somewhat rectified, will eventually lead to the destruction of the old campanile. Previous attempts to stabilize the tower have only caused further problems. In 1838, the ground around the south side was dug into and removed to expose the exterior, but the resulting hole eventually filled with water and caused greater damage. Then, in 1934, the Italian dictator Benito Mussolini ordered that exploratory soundings be taken around it. But those efforts caused the campanile to tilt even more quickly. Further instability has been caused by the lowering of the water table beneath the tower. As a result, uncontrolled pumping of groundwater is now prohibited.

Even visits by tourists cannot be tolerated. Pisa's most famous site can no longer be entered and climbed and thus further weakened.

Today, the tower is a full 17 feet out of plumb, a situation that puts immense stresses on its lower levels. Workers have been strapping steel cables to the tower's lower part in a stopgap effort to keep it from buckling under the strain. Numerous international experts also feel the strain while trying—so far in vain—to find a way that will somehow save the Leaning Tower of Pisa. It is unfortunate that these experts are not able to consult one of the city's favorite sons. The great Renaissance scientist Galileo grew up in Pisa and, in fact, climbed the tower to perform his free-fall gravity experiments. As someone who had wanted to understand gravity, perhaps he would have enjoyed trying to combat the very force that at last may topple Pisa's remarkable Leaning Tower.

Campo dei Miracoli, Pisa's famous square, deserves its name: In a miraculous victory against the odds, its Leaning Tower—begun 800 years ago and now inclined 17 feet out of plumb—continues to stand.

The world's natural wonders differ in a basic way from every other grouping of wonders: They were not made or greatly improved upon by humans. Mount Everest, the Great Barrier Reef, the Grand Canyon, Victoria Falls, the Harbor of Rio de Janeiro, Paricutín Volcano, and the Northern Lights do not cast a reflected glow over Man the Master. They humble humanity.

"Each one of us," wrote Aristotle, "adds a little to our understanding of Nature, and from all the facts assembled arises a certain grandeur." In the case of these wonders, our sense of grandeur has always preceded our understanding of their nature. Most of them are products of geologic forces that stretch back millions of years. But the field explaining their origin and formation, plate tectonics, is a youthful science; its insights, recent. The same holds true of ecology, which is beginning to tease apart the Great Barrier Reef's complex living web. To unlock secrets of the Northern Lights, scientists are using modern solar physics.

Though well known to local native peoples for millennia, most wonders on this list came to the notice of the Western world relatively recently. Mount Everest, for example, wasn't identified as the world's tallest peak until 1852, and its exact height is periodically disputed to this day.

As to the Grand Canyon, the leader of the U. S. government's first official expedition there, in 1857, told the War Department that it was "altogether valueless.... Ours has been the first, and will doubtless be the last, party of whites to visit this profitless locality." Elsewhere in his report, Lt. Joseph C. Ives rhapsodized about the canyon's magnificence, but he could not foresee that splendor alone would attract millions of visitors a year.

Today, for more and more people around the world, the canyon and other natural wonders are places of pilgrimage, where awe is its own reward.

SEVEN NATURAL WONDERS of the WORLD

....

by Leslie Allen

Snow swathes Isis Temple, one of several sandstone buttes chiseled from the Grand Canyon's North Rim. Nearly a mile below, the 300-foot-wide Colorado River appears threadlike.

Mount Everest

··········

Natural Wonders

Brooding black triangle, Mount Everest
disappears into clouds at 29,028 feet—
more than a mile above its sun-
drenched West Shoulder in Nepal.

To the Tibetan Sherpa people who have lived for centuries in its shadow, the world's tallest mountain is known as Bird of the Wind and Goddess Mother of the World. Nepal calls its crown jewel Sagarmatha, or "sky head." To the Western world, one word that conveys a supreme challenge says it all: Everest.

At 29,028 feet, Everest towers over its neighbors in the world's loftiest range, the Himalaya. "Its edge came leaping up at an angle of about 70 degrees and ended nowhere," wrote English mountaineer George Leigh Mallory in 1921. The peak is constantly buffeted by the jet stream—the high-altitude, high-speed current of air pushing weather systems across Central Asia. During the summer monsoon, a prodigious amount of snow falls in the Himalaya, and it almost never melts above 21,000 feet. Instead, the sheer weight of the snow causes it to fracture into massive blocks that suddenly roar down the slopes in avalanches.

The word "Himalaya" comes from a Sanskrit expression meaning "abode of snow." But the name actually encompasses three distinct ranges that arc across some 1,500 miles of the Indian subcontinent's northern fringes. From south to north, they form an ascending staircase,

Everest's "unscalable" East Face (above) yields a summit route in 1983, 30 years after Edmund Hillary and Tenzing Norgay first conquered the peak from the south. Chinese climbers forged a northern route up the mountain in 1960. On the East Face (opposite), tents perch on the edge of oblivion.

beginning with the Siwalik Range's low lush slopes and culminating in Everest at the Greater Himalaya's far end, between Nepal and Tibet.

Mount Everest began its existence about 325 million years ago in an ancient sea. About 60 million years ago, the tectonic plate carrying India was moving northward. Colliding with the Eurasian plate, it forced the floor of the Tethys Sea against the Asian landmass, squeezing it and thrusting it upward, causing it to crack. Its lightweight sediments and rock crumpled upward, giving rise to the Himalaya some 25 million years ago. As mountains go, the Himalaya are young and still growing. Deep beneath Tibet, the Indian plate continues its wedgelike northward drive, raising the Himalaya about two inches a year.

The highest peak for perhaps half a million years, Everest has been known as such for less than a century

"Because it is there." Legendary climber George Leigh Mallory's famous explanation of Mount Everest's allure still resonates for teams of mountaineers seeking to challenge this difficult and dangerous symbol of human achievement.

and a half. Sir George Everest, Surveyor General of India between 1830 and 1843, had supervised the Great Trigonometrical Survey of India and had overseen the construction of geodetic stations in northern India to measure the Himalaya. But Nepal, suspicious of British intentions,

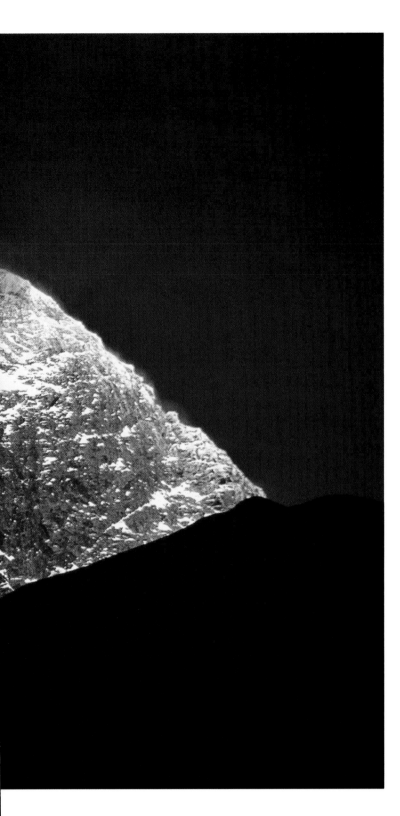

from the field survey. In 1865, XV became Everest in tribute to the surveyor general's pioneering mapping work.

"Can Mount Everest be climbed?" asked British surgeon and mountaineer Clinton Dent in an 1890s article published in *Nineteenth Century* magazine. But the answer to his rhetorical question—that the climb was "humanly possible"—awaited trial until the 1920s for political reasons. Neither Tibet nor Nepal welcomed a mountaineering party until 1921, when a British reconnaissance team went through Tibet to reach the North Col, at almost 23,000 feet. A year later, some of the same climbers, including George Mallory, tried for the summit, but when an avalanche on the North Col killed seven Sherpa porters, the expedition was called off. In 1924, on a third expedition, Mallory and his young companion, Sandy Irvine, were spotted "going strong for the top" when they disappeared forever in a swirl of mist. What became of them? As he searched the gale-swept heights for them, Noel Odell, another climber, thought Everest "seemed to look down with cold indifference on me, mere puny man, and howl derision in wind gusts at my petition to yield up its secret."

In the 1930s and '40s, Everest remained, in the public imagination, nature's last unconquered stronghold. Flags had been planted on the North and South Poles, while Everest was still the unyielding "third pole." It was a polar cap with reduced oxygen levels, set at an elevation physiologically antithetical to human endeavor. "Nothing but the most perfect conditions of weather and snow offer the slightest chance of success," declared British Everest veteran Eric Shipton. He was the ablest climber of the time, but he was replaced as leader of the 1953 assault on Everest. For that ascent, the conditions were right, the planning and organization were impeccable, and the climbers were among the Commonwealth's best. At 11:30 a.m. on May 29, Edmund Hillary, a New Zealand beekeeper, and Tenzing Norgay, a Sherpa resident in India, reached the summit. "My initial feelings were of relief," wrote Hillary, "relief that there were no more steps to cut, no more ridges to traverse and no more humps to tantalize us with hopes of success.... The ridge had taken us two and a half hours, but it seemed like a lifetime."

Since 1953, hundreds of climbers from dozens of countries have matched the feat of Hillary and Norgay. But Everest has also claimed about 150 lives over the years. The fruits of technology, including improved equipment, have not lowered the toll: 1996 proved a more lethal climbing year than any before it, with 15 fatalities. But as Everest's lure spreads like a contagious dream, little has changed since George Mallory gave his famous explanation for its pull: "Because it is there."

turned down his request to work inside that country. The surveyor general retired to England, and others carried on the survey, marking one tall mountain as XV.

The discovery that the mountain overtopped all others was made in 1852, following a cross-check of figures

The Great Barrier Reef

....

Natural Wonders

Australia's Great Barrier Reef, a giant maze of coral islands and individual reefs, protects the northeast coast from ocean waves and shelters thousands of fish and shellfish species.

Stretching for 1,250 miles along the northeast coast of Queensland, Australia, the Great Barrier Reef is the largest grouping of reefs in the world. At least 2,900 individual coral reefs, along with some 300 islets and 600 continental islands, are sprinkled across about 135,000 square miles of ocean, an area that is larger than Great Britain and half the size of Texas.

For astronauts on the space shuttle, the Great Barrier Reef comes into clear focus as a long trail of white set against the whirling blue of the Coral Sea. Yet within its vastness are living worlds of astonishing minuteness. The Great Barrier Reef is made of—and has been constructed by—tiny, simple organisms: hard coral polyps. The reef's building blocks, polyps are tentacled animals bearing cylinder-like limestone skeletons. Single-celled plants called zooxanthellae remove wastes from the polyps and provide them with nutrients. And algae, like mortar, cements the skeletons of dead corals and other organisms, helping to consolidate the reef.

Bleached and brittle, reef walls represent the remains of millions of previous generations of hard corals. Only the colorful, topmost layer of the reef is a living community. Here, the branches of staghorn corals reach toward the surface; round yellow mushroom corals gleam; and sunlight dapples soft corals such as delicate sea fans and whips. Altogether, the Great Barrier Reef contains some 400 coral species. In turn, the corals continue to provide the underpinning of one of the world's most biologically diverse ecosystems, including at least 1,500 species of fish, 4,000 species of mollusks, 240 species of birds, and a variety of highly endangered species of different kinds.

Why and how so many living species thrive symbiotically on the Great Barrier Reef are questions that continue to elude scientific certainty. The maturity of the ecosystem is probably a crucial factor; the coral reef community is the oldest ecosystem in geologic history. By the Miocene epoch, about 28 million years ago, tectonic movement in this region had shifted northeastern Australia into tropical latitudes. The warmer climate and the clear and balmy waters were highly favorable to the development of coral reefs. Then, faulting or down-warping hollowed out a shallow marine basin where the corals could flourish.

Over millions of years, subsidence drowned much of the coastal area. But here and there, mountaintops poked above the water. These rocky peaks, now known as continental islands, much later gave rise to the offshore fringing reefs that are familiar to most visitors to the Great Barrier Reef.

By about 20 million years ago, the northernmost portions of the Great Barrier Reef were formed. Long, almost continuous ribbon reefs edge the continental shelf there; windward walls plunge a mile deep while leeward sides define a remote, shallow-water environment of varied reef forms and great biological richness. Ribbon reefs are gradually replaced by large, knoll-like platform reefs and many other coral formations as the continental shelf widens and the water deepens in the central and southern sections, which may be only about a million years old.

Creation, destruction, and re-creation—by tectonic movement, weather, tides, winds, and, increasingly, the hand of man—are ongoing forces along the Great Barrier Reef. If change is a watchword, diversity in all aspects defines this reef. Though neither a barrier for most of its length, nor a single entity, the entire reef system is no less than the greatest of the earth's living wonders. For more on the reef, see the "Underwater Wonders" chapter.

The Grand Canyon

··········

Natural Wonders

In the blink of an eye, canyon caprock gives way to Granite Gorge schists 1.7 billion years old. Iron oxides, fired by sunset, impart lavish shades of red and orange at South Rim's Yaki Point.

The Grand Canyon of the Colorado River is the largest gorge in the world—a 290-mile-long gash across the face of the Colorado Plateau in northern Arizona. Rim to rim, it measures up to 18 miles across, with an average width of 10 miles; its average depth is one mile. Within this Delaware-size area of eroded rock rise mountains higher than any in the eastern United States and the dark walls of gorges millions of years old. Agent of this scene, the Colorado River drops 2,200 feet over nearly 200 rapids as it roars through the canyon toward the Gulf of California.

Numbers, though, tell only part of the canyon's story and merely hint at the magic of its myriad hues, strata, spires, and gorges. The place is more than the sum of its parts—so much more that neither the eye nor the mind of the beholder can encompass more than a small part of it at one time. As John Wesley Powell, whose party in 1869 became the first to traverse the canyon by river, wrote, "You cannot see the Grand Canyon in one view, as if it were a changeless spectacle from which a curtain might be lifted."

At the canyon's bottom, a mile below the rim, the Colorado River slices through Granite Gorge, exposing some of the oldest rocks visible anywhere on the earth. Nearly two billion years old, the Vishnu schist is the gleaming black remnant of a once towering mountain range. Some 500 million years after it formed, vast rifting and faulting laid down the tilted, colorful sediments of the Grand Canyon Series atop the schist. Ten distinct layers of sandstone, limestone, and shale bespeak the advance and retreat of ancient seas, the building up and wearing down of mountains, the meandering of rivers over 600 million years.

At either rim, visitors today perch atop creamy Kaibab limestone cliffs studded with fossilized sponges, corals, snails, and shellfish that inhabited a warm inland sea 240 million years ago. Though rock layers once covered this ancient seabed, all geologic signs of the more recent Mesozoic and Cenozoic eras wore away eons ago.

Compared with the nearly two-billion-year process of deposition, erosion has set a brisk pace. The Grand Canyon itself is less than six million years old, created only since the Colorado River changed course and began

Mule-borne visitors, circa 1917, pause for a Kolb Brothers photograph (above). In his 73 years of working at the Grand Canyon, Emery Kolb estimated 1.5 million "faces and mules" posed for him.

Scarlet monkeyflowers rim stream-fed Elves Chasm (opposite), one of the canyon's hidden jewels.

flowing through the ancestral Colorado Plateau. In just two million years, the river sliced to within 500 feet of its current depth. Wind, rain, snow, heat, and cold have helped the process along. So has the flow of hundreds of tributaries, many of which are dry washes, filled intermittently by snowmelt and summer thunderstorms. Over eons these streams have created "a composite of thousands, of tens of thousands, of gorges," as Powell marveled. "Every one of these...is a world of beauty in itself."

The Grand Canyon is not only a slice of North America's geologic history but also a cross section of ecozones.

Natural Wonders

Between rim and river, travelers find the same variety of ecological regions they would encounter on a trip from Canada to Mexico—from the snowy evergreen woods of the boreal zone to the arid depths of the lower Sonoran, where summer temperatures soar above 100°F and tenacious shrubs like creosote and ocotillo predominate. In all, the Grand Canyon provides rich and diverse habitat for more than 400 vertebrate species and 1,500 plants.

The human presence here stretches back at least 4,000 years, beginning with hunter-gatherers who deposited delicate split-willow animal figures in limestone caves. Before disappearing about A.D. 1150, ancient Pueblo peoples who had lived in and around the canyon for a millennium or more left a rich legacy of pottery, baskets, pictographs, and granaries and other structures in thousands of sites. The Havasupai people in the region today trace their presence back hundreds of years.

During the 20th century, humans have had a far more profound impact on the Grand Canyon than in all of the past. By 1900, the canyon was already a well-known destination, thanks to written accounts by explorers and scientists and to the glowing canvases of artist Thomas Moran. And after Grand Canyon National Park was established in 1919, the number of visitors continued to increase exponentially: About five million people now visit the canyon each year by car, on foot, atop mules, on motorized rafts, and in helicopters. Some of the human impact, such as the view-marring haze drifting in from power plants and urban centers, has been indirect. In 1963, the Glen Canyon Dam ended the Colorado River's free flow at the Grand Canyon's entrance, and that single action has changed the canyon more than any other event in human times.

To John Wesley Powell a century earlier, the sound of rushing water in the canyon was "a symphony of multitudinous melodies." But with the flick of a switch, the ebb and flood that had shaped the canyon's complex ecosystems over countless millennia were halted. Since 1963, the ecological richness of the canyon has sharply declined. In 1996, officials opened Glen Canyon Dam for a weeklong test flood designed to imitate natural flooding. While it failed to right the ecological imbalances that had taken hold, the event marked an important acknowledgment that nature's imperatives, though easily tampered with, have their own logic.

At Nankoweap, visitors sit in front of a granary built into the Redwall by ancient Pueblo peoples. Thousands of archaeological sites attest to the long presence of humans in the Grand Canyon.

Victoria Falls

....

Natural Wonders

Mile-wide curtain of water plummets off a basaltic precipice into the slotlike gorge 355 feet below, as the placid upper Zambezi River transforms itself into a torrent at Victoria Falls.

Kololo invaders, forging northward into the heart of Africa, called the falls Mosi-oa-Tunya—"smoke that thunders." To Scottish missionary David Livingstone, exploring the Zambezi River in 1855, they were "the most wonderful sight I had witnessed in Africa." The first European to see the falls, Livingstone named them for his queen, Victoria.

Victoria Falls dashed Livingstone's hope of finding a navigable route eastward to the Indian Ocean. But his account of the breathtaking spectacle he witnessed from a small island at the top of the falls was riveting. "Creeping with awe to the verge, I peered down into a large rent which had been made from bank to bank of the broad Zambesi...." he wrote. "In looking down into the fissure on the right of the island, one sees nothing but a dense white cloud which, at the time we visited the spot, had two bright rainbows on it.... The snow-white sheet seemed like myriads of small comets rushing in one direction, each of which left behind its nucleus rays of foam."

Concerned that he might be accused of exaggeration, Livingstone instead veered toward serious underestimates of the falls' magnitude. Since then, accurate measurements have confirmed what early witnesses instinctively knew: Victoria Falls ranks as a superlative among superlatives. Located along the border of present-day Zimbabwe and Zambia, the mile-wide falls form the world's largest-known curtain of falling water. They are more than twice as wide and twice as deep as Niagara Falls. Thundering from bank to bank over a sheer precipice of basalt, the Zambezi River plunges as much as 355 feet.

Flowing eastward through a wide, flat-bottomed valley above the falls, the river moves languidly, eddying around small verdant islands without gathering speed; only rolling thunder and thickening mist signal the falls just ahead. But instead of falling into an open basin, the river plunges into a narrow chasm, between 80 and 240 feet wide, that parallels the falls. The Zambezi then zigzags through seven more slender gorges. Here the river is a raging torrent penned in by walls 400 to 800 feet high. These walls, the beginning of Batoka Gorge, slice through the basalt plateau for another 60 miles.

What could have created the falls and the sheer-walled clefts below them? Livingstone himself speculated that a cataclysmic event suddenly split the earth's crust, and the Zambezi simply poured into the fracture. But modern geology instead fingers the long-range changes and global links of plate tectonics—the movement of huge slabs of the earth's crust.

Perhaps 150 million years ago, molten upheavals lifted parts of Africa's crust, shaping the land into broad domes. Southern Africa, including the area that is now Zambia and Zimbabwe, became one of the domes. As stresses built, cracks and fissures opened in the ground and molten rock poured out. Great sheets of lava blanketed an area stretching from the Atlantic to the Indian Ocean and eventually turned into basalt. As the lava cooled, cracks may have formed over the area—some on an east-west axis and others on a north-south axis—and these became the falls and gorges millions of years afterward. Today, the falls mark a right angle to the river just beyond the spot where the Zambezi swings to a north-south course.

Relentlessly scraping and gouging, the falls are slowly but surely retreating northward. Just during humanity's early presence in the area, starting thousands of years ago, the northern lips of several downstream gorges were themselves full-fledged Victoria Falls. Gradually, the pounding water undermined them one by one. Over the next 40,000 years, the fall line will keep

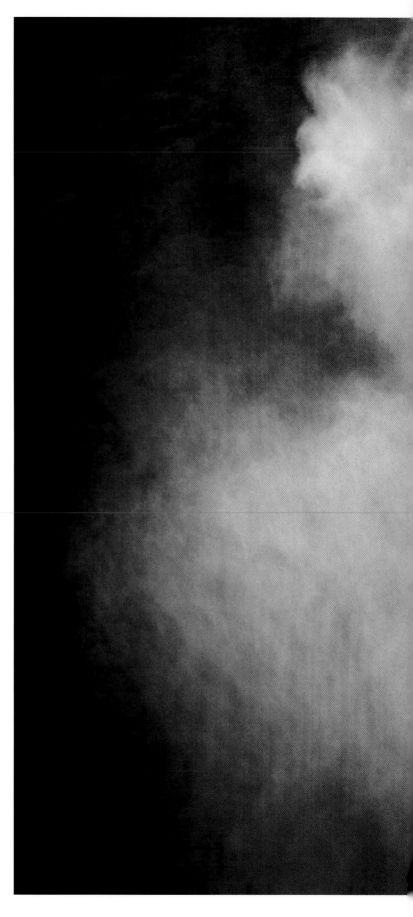

"A large rent" to explorer David Livingstone, the falls' main chasm displays east-west fissuring caused by shifting tectonic plates. The Kololo people called the spray (right) "smoke that thunders," a presence often dense enough to hide Victoria Falls from view.

moving back, creating similar waterfalls, until it reaches the point where the river flows east. From there, it will continue upstream, forming narrow waterfalls.

Anyone who sees Victoria Falls today views a scene much changed since David Livingstone came here. Visitors, roads, and hotels abound. People line up to bungee jump, take helicopter trips, and ride the whitewater. All of the individual cataracts—Main Falls, Rainbow Falls, and Devil's Cataract, for example—and other natural features bear English names. Below the cataracts, Victoria Falls Bridge is a busy international boundary linking Zambia and Zimbabwe. But while trails now thread the banks of the Zambezi River, no metal railings have been set up that would protect sightseers or mar the view, and no floodlights illuminate the falls at night.

Aiming to preserve the physical environment, Zambia's Mosi-oa-Tunya National Park and Zimbabwe's Victoria Falls National Park shelter a breathtaking trove of living things. Some 500 plant species, including a high number never seen elsewhere, blanket the Zambezi's banks, stud its palmy islands, and cling tenaciously to its sheer-walled gorges. And a variety of large and small mammals, reptiles, birds, and fish still inhabit the fragile realm surrounding Victoria Falls.

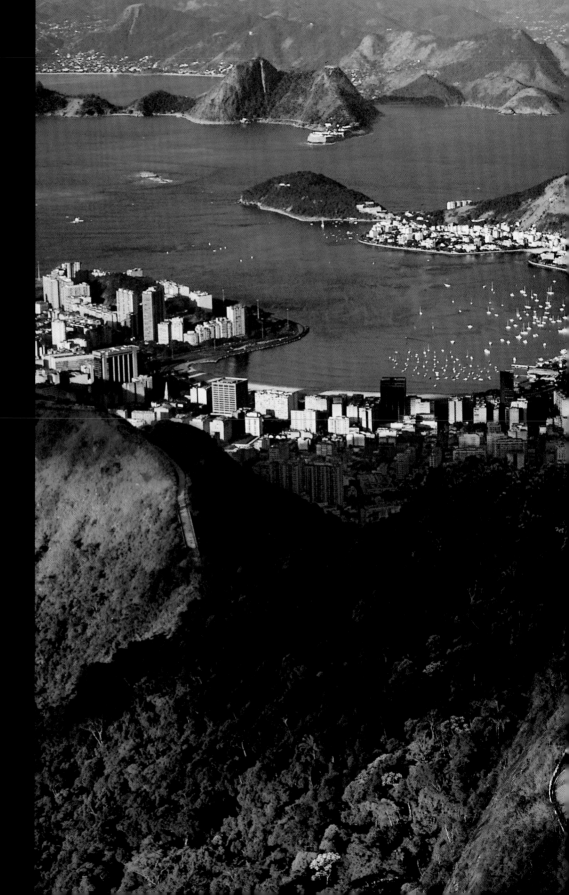

The Harbor of Rio de Janeiro

· · · · · · · · · ·

Natural Wonders

Atop Corcovado Mountain, Christ the Redeemer soars above Rio de Janeiro. Beyond boat-flecked Botafogo Bay, Sugarloaf stands sentinel at the opening to a balloon-shaped harbor.

Visible from most parts of Rio de Janeiro's populous Southern Zone, the figure of Christ—arms open 92 feet wide—remains the city's best-loved symbol. The statue's serene expression contrasts sharply with the frenzy of pre-Lenten revelry swirling far below during Rio's four-day Carnival (opposite).

At the beginning of the 16th century, the Portuguese explorers who sailed down Brazil's coast kept track of their discoveries, and the days of the year, by naming the former for the latter. On New Year's Day, 1502, they glided toward a narrow opening in the coastline, guarded by fabulously shaped mountains. Beyond this entrance lay a body of water stretching 20 miles inland. Convinced that they had reached the mouth of a great river, they named the area River of the First of January.

The large waterway was not a river; it was an island-studded bay that the Tamoio people had long before named Guanabara—"arm of the sea." Nearly five centuries later, both the native and European names persist. But now, instead of caravels and dugouts, supertankers and yachts glide across the magnificent balloon-shaped harbor of Guanabara Bay. No longer a tropical wilderness teeming with tapirs and jaguars, the bay's western shores now hold a roaring metropolis called Rio de Janeiro—the River of January.

The great bay that looked like a river was only one of many illusions that Rio held. Europeans called the smaller bay of Botafogo, under Sugarloaf, a "lake"; the Tamoio themselves named Guanabara Bay's eastern edge Niterói, meaning "hidden waters." For early European voyagers, it was as though, when Rio hove into view, the curtain rose on a stage set with such strange, striking shapes and forms that virtually everything looked like something else. Charles Darwin, during the voyage of the *Beagle,* wrote from Rio in 1832 that "every form, every shade, so completely surpasses in magnificence all that the European has ever beheld in his own country, that he knows not how to express his feelings. The general effect frequently recalled to my mind the gayest scenery of the Opera-house or the great theatres."

Guarding the entrance to the bay, the naked and lopsided mountain the Portuguese called Pão de Açúcar evoked the sugarloaves fashioned on the island of Madeira. They called the highest mountain Corcovado—"the hunchback"—for its humped profile. Today, a statue of Christ the Redeemer crowns the 2,300-foot-high peak.

Whether stark, isolated cones or undulating rows of ridges resembling the breakers on the beaches below, Rio's peaks and hills are outliers of the Serra do Mar. Also called the Great Escarpment, this ancient gneiss-granite mountain chain rises in the state of Bahia, to the north, and stretches 1,500 miles to Rio Grande do Sul, Brazil's southernmost state. Plunging straight into the water, the mountains add breathtaking drama to Rio's harbor, but to early would-be settlers they posed a daunting obstacle.

Though Rio boasted the finest harbor anyone could hope to find, the shores of Guanabara Bay had practically no flat land; what little there was usually lay beneath pestilent swamps. As a European settlement, Rio got off to a sluggish start: More than half a century after the Portuguese named it, the River of January held only a small outpost of Antarctic France. The site of that fortress settlement, Villegaignon Island, is now the location of Brazil's naval academy. Portuguese colonists finally dislodged their French rival in 1567, but well into the 17th century Rio remained a backwater. Sugar mills sprang up around the bay, and cane fields rustled where jumbo jets now scream across Ilha do Governador—"governor's island"—the bay's largest island and the site of Rio's international airport.

Sugar, a prized commodity in Europe, gave the harbor its first commercial purpose. Then, as the 18th century began, gold was discovered inland; along Rio's quays, ships loaded the treasure for the royal coffers of Portugal, whose colony Brazil remained until 1889. Coffee, introduced to Brazil by Jesuit missionaries, followed. But as more ships bearing Brazil's raw wealth sailed out of the bay, others sailed in bearing African slaves bound for plantations and mines. Although outlawed in 1830, the Brazilian slave trade flourished into the 1850s.

Undulating sidewalk mosaic laps Copacabana Beach (above). At right, Dois Irmãos—"two brothers"— and flat-topped Gávea—"topsail"—offer angular counterpoint to the curve of Ipanema and Leblon.

When Brazil gained its independence from Portugal, with Rio as its capital, the city's population was around half a million. Today, Rio is no longer the national capital—Brasilia is—but the city is 20 times larger, having exploded far beyond its original bayside neighborhoods. The city of Niterói, on Guanabara Bay's eastern shore, now seems more suburb than distinct metropolis following the opening of an eight-mile bridge linking it to Rio.

The bay's vastness has been shrinking in more literal ways, too. With usable land at a premium, landfill has twice altered Guanabara Bay's contours. In the 1920s and again in the 1960s, small hills that once had been home to Rio's earliest settlers were sluiced through pipes to create bayfill. The new land now anchors an airport, a six-lane highway, parkland and beaches, the city's modern art museum, and other 20th-century landmarks as Rio looks to its great bay for elbowroom.

Natural Wonders
....
129

Paricutín Volcano

....

Natural Wonders

Enfant terrible, two-month-old Paricutín already nears 500 feet. In this, its cineritic phase, a billowing column of ash and vapor turned day to dusk more than a hundred miles away.

On the afternoon of February 20, 1943, Dionisio Pulido, a farmer in the Mexican state of Michoacán, was readying his fields for spring sowing when the ground nearby opened in a fissure about 150 feet long. "I then felt a thunder," he recalled later, "the trees trembled, and it was then I saw how, in the hole, the ground swelled and raised itself 2 or 2 ½ meters high, and a kind of smoke or fine dust—gray, like ashes—began to rise up in a portion of the crack.... Immediately more smoke began to rise, with a hiss or whistle, loud and continuous; and there was a smell of sulphur. I then became greatly frightened and tried to help unyoke one of the ox teams."

Virtually under the farmer's feet, a volcano was being born. Pulido and the handful of other witnesses fled. By the next morning, when he returned, the cone had grown to a height of 30 feet and was "hurling out rocks with great violence." During the day, the cone grew another 120 feet. That night, incandescent bombs blew more than 1,000 feet up into the darkness, and a slaglike mass of lava rolled over Pulido's cornfields.

The scientific world was almost as stunned as the hapless farmer himself by the volcano's sudden appearance. Around the world, volcanic eruptions are commonplace, but the birth of an entirely new volcano, marked by the arrival at the earth's surface of a distinct vent from the magma chamber, is genuinely rare. In North America, only two new volcanoes have appeared in historic times. One of them was western Mexico's Jorullo, born in 1759 some 50 miles southeast of Dionisio Pulido's property. The second, born about 183 years later in Pulido's field, was named Paricutín for a nearby village that it eventually destroyed.

Paricutín and Jorullo both rose in an area known for its volcanoes. Called the Mexican Volcanic Belt, the region stretches about 700 miles from east to west across southern Mexico. Geologists say that eruptions began there at least ten million years ago. Over eons all of this eruptive activity deposited a layer of volcanic rock some 6,000 feet thick, creating a high and fertile plateau. During summer months, the heights snag moisture-laden breezes from the Pacific Ocean; rich farmland, in turn, has made this belt the most populous region in Mexico.

Though the region already boasted three of the country's four largest cities—Mexico City, Puebla, and Guadalajara—the area around Paricutín, some 200 miles west of the capital, was still a peaceful backwater inhabited by Tarascan Indians in the early 1940s. Its gently rolling landscape, in a zone that had experienced almost no volcanic activity during historic times, was one of Mexico's loveliest. Although hundreds of extinct cinder cones rose around the small valleys, the only eruption in human memory had been that of distant Jorullo.

The Tarascan had no folk legends concerning volcanic eruptions in the area. But when Paricutín came into their lives, they saw events, in retrospect, that foretold the cataclysm. The first event was a sacrilege: the 1941 destruction of a large wooden cross on a hillside. The second one hinted at biblical retribution: a plague of locusts in 1942. When 1943 began, so did the third sign: a series of earthquakes; these were preceded, said one man, by "many noises in the center of the earth."

On February 19, the day before the volcano began to erupt, some 300 earthquakes shook the ground. On February 22, with the new cone rising and fiery skyrockets descending, the first of many geologists who would monitor

After reaching 1,353 feet in 1952, Paricutín died young (right). Its legacy included a lava-engulfed village church to the north (above).

and map Paricutín's behavior over the next nine years arrived. From then on, Paricutín was under constant observation: It yielded a trove of information, including unique, fleeting glimpses of ephemeral features.

New volcanic phenomena and processes were sometimes obliterated almost as soon as they were recorded, especially during Paricutín's first year of violent, explosive growth and change. In that year, the cone topped 1,100 feet, four-fifths of its final height; explosions echoed all over the state of Michoacán; ash snowed on faraway Mexico City; and almost all of the vegetation for miles around the crater was destroyed .

During the summer of 1943, probably the volcano's most violent period, lava rose to about 50 feet below the crater's rim. That fall, a new vent opened explosively at the cone's base, fountaining lava high into the sky. Lava finally destroyed the nearby villages the following year, but most villagers had seen their livelihoods disappear long before that.

Over the next years, lava flows continued with little interruption. But in February of 1952, almost exactly nine years after Paricutín was born, the volcano experienced its last major spasm of activity. By then, villages and farms had been relocated with government assistance. The new Bracero Program drew many of the displaced farmers to California for seasonal agricultural work. One of them was Dionisio Pulido, who, it was said, left behind on his property a sign that read, "This volcano owned and operated by Dionisio Pulido."

The Northern Lights

··········

Natural Wonders

Celestial ribbons unfurl over Denali
National Park in Alaska. In Inuit
tradition, they represent torches held
by spirits to guide the souls of the dead
down eternity's corridor.

"And now from the far-away western horizon a fiery serpent writhed itself up over the sky, shining brighter and brighter as it came. It split into three, all brilliantly glittering. Then the colours changed. The serpent to the south turned almost ruby-red, with spots of yellow; the one in the middle yellow, and the one to the north, greenish white. Sheaves of rays swept along the side of the serpents, driven through the ether-like waves before a storm wind."

His ship frozen hard into polar pack ice, Norwegian explorer Fridtjof Nansen might understandably have whiled away the long, dark Arctic winter with fanciful visions. But what Nansen saw writhing across the black sky one night in 1893 was an entirely real display of one of nature's most spectacular phenomena: the aurora borealis, or northern lights.

The name brings together two mythological deities—Aurora, the Roman goddess of the dawn, and Boreas, Greek god of the north wind—to describe an event witnessed mostly at night in the high northerly latitudes.

An identical phenomenon, the aurora australis, occurs in the high latitudes of the Southern Hemisphere, a region that has always been much more sparsely inhabited than the planet's northern reaches. Only a few eyewitness accounts of the aurora australis were available before 20th-century explorers arrived in Antarctica.

By contrast, the flowing ribbons, sky-filling swirls, otherworldly glow, gossamer veils, and brilliant rays of the aurora borealis are a regular presence that has awed and terrified northern peoples for thousands of years. To Finns the aurora was "fox fire" sparked by glistening fur. Some Alaskan Inuit saw the dancing souls of deer, seals, salmon, and beluga; others believed that if they whistled the lights might snatch them away. The Athabascan saw messages from their dead, the "sky dwellers." The lights' mysterious movements inspired whimsical metaphors such as "nimble men" and "merry dancers," marionettes and polkas. But from ancient China to 20th-century Europe, people have also seen in the night sky clashing swords and bloody armies—portents of conflagration.

For a long time, scientists offered almost as many interpretations of the northern lights as did the traditional peoples who observed them. Then, starting in the 19th century, studies of earth's magnetism and the sun's workings, along with the careful observations of polar explorers, began to unlock the aurora's mysteries.

The aurora arises in the roiling turbulence of the sun. More than 100,000 times hotter than boiling water, the sun's interior chops the atoms that form solar gases into a thin stream of electrically charged particles—protons and electrons. Both matter and energy, this stream continuously erupts from the sun and is called the solar wind. Two or three days after bursting from the sun's surface at speeds of up to 500 miles a second, the solar wind reaches the earth, 93 million miles away.

The solar wind has the force to swiftly annihilate life on the earth. What stops it from doing so is the shielding power of the planet's magnetic field, reaching out more than 40,000 miles into space. Like the earth, the sun is also a mighty magnet, and the solar wind carries fragments

Colliding with atmospheric gases, charged solar particles create an infinite variety of auroral displays. Variations in altitude, type of gas, intensity of the solar wind, and position of the observer affect the appearance of an aurora. Seen from directly below, the rayed arcs of a corona (far left) resemble a sunburst. Oxygen glows greenish more than 250 miles up, but red at lower altitudes. From 80 to 100 miles up, nitrogen molecules bombarded by solar particles shine violet and blue; between 60 and 80 miles up, nitrogen and oxygen may both produce rosy pinks.

of its magnetic field. As solar particles crash into the planet's magnetic field, the fields repel each other.

Though most of the solar wind harmlessly sideswipes the magnetic shield, small streams of solar particles do manage to become trapped, spiraling down toward the planet's north and south magnetic poles. As they tumble, beams of electrons spread, ripple, and swirl, and yet their movements remain invisible. But when the solar wind

Eye in the sky, the satellite-borne Earth Camera captures the auroral oval over northern polar regions from 25,000 miles out in space. Glow from the sun's lighting of the upper atmosphere creates a large yellow crescent at the top of the image.

A dancing veil of light above Alaska's Chugach Mountains, the aurora borealis frames comet Hale-Bopp as it passes through the solar system.

hits the upper reaches of the ionosphere and encounters atmospheric gases, it starts churning the thin soup of oxygen and nitrogen there. Marvelous shapes and flowing patterns begin to appear. Electrons bouncing around among atoms of oxygen create a greenish glow between about 250 and 600 miles above the earth's surface and a red glow much lower. Nitrogen molecules hit by solar wind may shine bright pink, or blue and violet, depending upon their distance from the surface.

The ever changing dance of lights belies the aurora's permanence. Though only parts of it can be seen at any time, and almost never during the day, the aurora borealis forms a 2,000-mile-wide auroral oval above the magnetic north pole day in and day out, year after year.

What *can* dramatically change the oval are the occasional spikes in solar activity that turn the solar wind into a raging hurricane. Then, for a few days, the auroral oval flows toward the Equator and treats sky-gazers as far south as Mexico to midnight extravaganzas. At the same time, electromagnetic disturbances intensify, with overloaded power lines and scrambled communications serving to remind us of the force behind the celestial fireworks.

Describing the sea and his deep fascination with it, noted marine explorer Jacques-Yves Cousteau wrote: "It is all strange, unearthly, and yet familiar. Strange because the sea, once it casts its spell, holds one in its net of wonders forever."

Today, more and more people are being drawn to the underwater realm. Divers are strapping on scuba gear or climbing into submersibles so that they can encounter exotic marine species, view seafloor volcanoes, or marvel at intricate reef formations and their biologically diverse ecosystems.

Coral reefs, like many of the wonders named in this book, are structures built by living organisms. But they are also made of living things: tiny creatures called coral polyps. Second only to tropical rain forests in biodiversity, coral reefs provide homes for thousands of species. Unfortunately, they are at risk all around the world.

To promote awareness of the fragile marine ecosystem, CEDAM International—an organization dedicated to conservation, education, diving, and marine research—began the Seven Underwater Wonders of the World Project in 1989. The message was simple: If underwater wonders aren't protected, they will be lost forever. After considering sites around the world, CEDAM chose Palau, the Belize Barrier Reef, the Galápagos Islands, the Northern Red Sea, Lake Baikal, the Great Barrier Reef, and the Deep-sea Vents. Each was selected on the basis of its natural beauty, unique marine life, scientific research value, environmental significance, geologic significance, and whether it is representative of an overall area.

By focusing on these seven sites, CEDAM hopes to promote the protection of all underwater wonders. "We are the first generation to explore the wonders of the underwater world," says George Page, host of the public television series *Nature.* "Let's hope we are not the last."

SEVEN UNDERWATER WONDERS of the WORLD

··········

by Rick Sammon

On the lookout for predators, a two-inch-long two-bar clownfish snuggles among the tentacles of a sea anemone, a sedentary animal related to jellyfish and corals. Fierce clownfish attack divers and fish many times their size.

Palau

· · · · · · · · · ·

Underwater Wonders

ding over dead-calm water, visitors
owerboats glimpse Palau's Seventy
slands, the peaks of submerged
nic mountains. In the clear, shallow
ters, snorkelers and divers often
unter turtles, sharks, and stingrays.

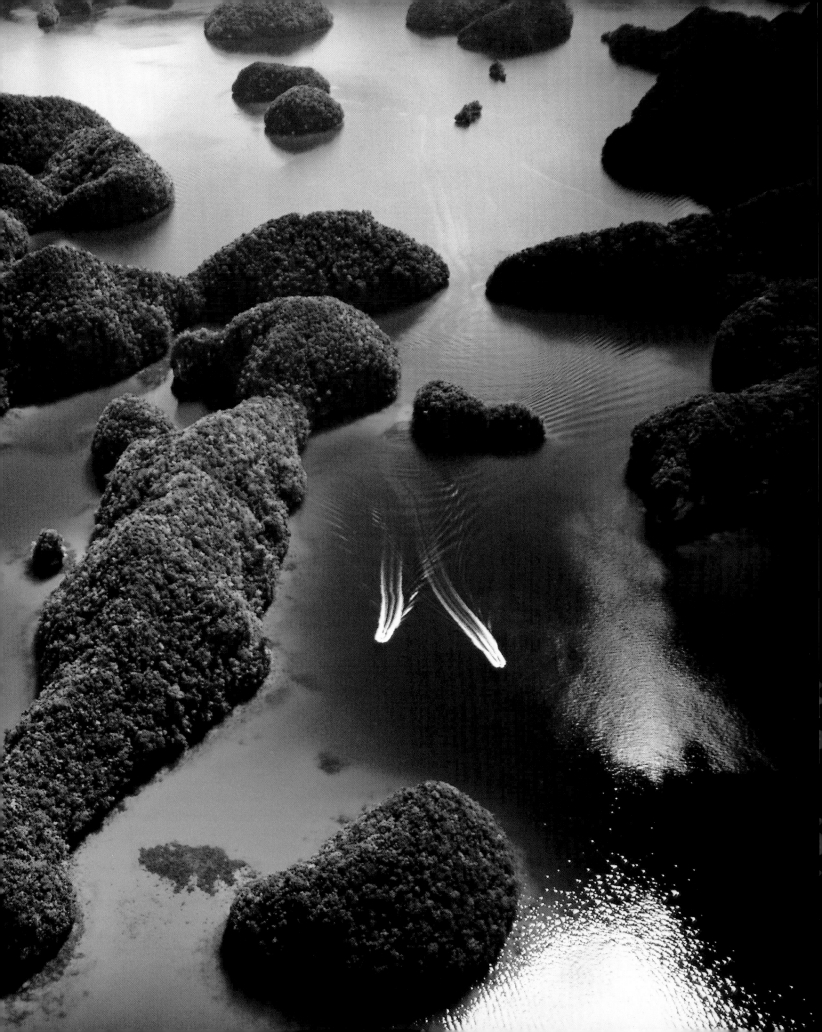

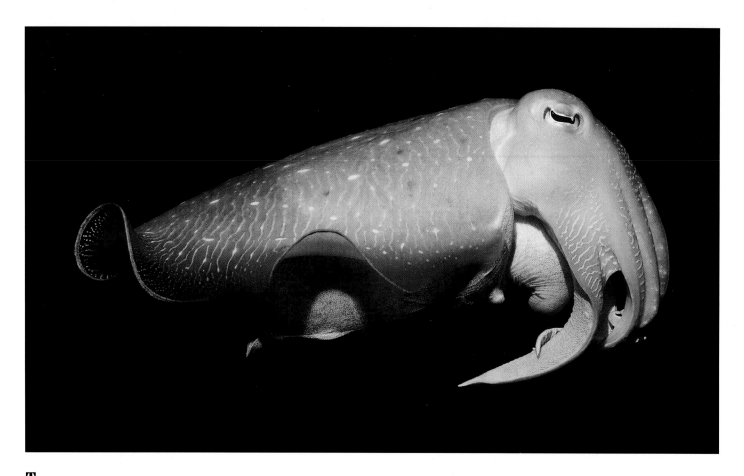

The warm waters of Palau, a small archipelago in the Pacific Ocean, hold perhaps the richest and most biologically diverse coral reefs on the planet. In this "cradle of diversity," marine biologists have recorded 700 species of corals and 1,500 species of fish.

Palau's coral reefs began to grow millions of years ago when coral polyps colonized submerged volcanic mountains. The tiny polyps produced a material that cemented them in place. Side by side, they built hard, external skeletons around their soft bodies, and when they died, other corals built skeletons on top of them. Geologic forces eventually raised the coral-topped mountains above the sea, and all the exposed corals died. In time, new colonies built more reefs on the islands' undersea slopes.

Today, divers swimming over the coral gardens of Ngemelis Island are moved by nature's artistry and creativity. The top of this reef, just a few feet below the surface, resembles wildflowers swaying in a breeze. Here, soft coral trees and bushes seem to have been painted in stunning shades of red, green, yellow, and orange.

Among the many fish species fluttering around gracefully are yellow butterflyfish, blue-headed wrasses, and emperor angelfish—black-masked and striped. Not so graceful, though, is the mango-size puffer, a fish that

Hovering over a reef, a cuttlefish (above) reacts to predators, prey, and potential mates by changing its color pattern. The animal's brain sends signals to pigment sacs located on its soft, fleshy body.

Delicate appendages help a feather star perch on a sea fan (opposite). Early underwater explorers incorrectly called this flowerlike animal a plant.

sucks in water when startled and inflates its body to the size of a football. Sharp spikes stick out in all directions and are quite a deterrent to potential predators. Another cumbersome swimmer is the pear-size trunkfish, whose tough, trunklike body is difficult for predators to chew.

Nestled among the Ngemelis corals are giant clams. These two- to three-foot-long creatures, depicted in early movies as being able to grab divers' feet, feed harmlessly on plankton—not divers. And poking ever so slightly out of cracks in the corals are green and red brittle stars. Related to sea stars, these animals grow arms that break off easily if bitten by predators or touched by scuba divers. Brittle stars hide until sundown, but at night they crawl out, spread their arms, and feed on plankton.

Sometimes the best way to observe fish is to find a sandy patch, settle down, and wait, letting them get

accustomed to you. And a good technique for finding a particular kind of fish is to look from right to left, rather than left to right—the usual way in which people view things. Looking in this manner slows down the viewing process and increases the odds of sighting an animal.

Not difficult to spot are watermelon-size cuttlefish hovering in the water. Related to the octopus and squid, these members of the cephalopod group can change their colors, patterns, and shapes so that they sometimes look like floating plants or free-swimming octopuses, their arms tickling unseen objects. Another master at deception is the crocodilefish. A lie-in-wait predator, this three-foot-long fish has an uncanny resemblance to its reptilian namesake.

One of the greatest underwater shows on earth can be seen at Blue Corner, a part of the archipelago named for the deep blue quality of its water. Here, currents strong enough to rip the mask from a diver's face bring in a healthy supply of plankton, a food source that attracts unicornfish, tangs, and other plankton-eaters. In turn, these fish attract huge schools of predators, including sharks and jacks. A school of jacks can number 300 or 400 and be so dense that it nearly blocks the sunlight, creating the effect of an underwater eclipse. Blue Corner also attracts manta rays and eagle rays. With wingspans of several feet, these large plankton-feeders have few predators and can feed leisurely without having to worry about the ever present sharks patrolling the reef.

At Blue Corner, the currents are so fast that a diver's encounter with pelagic fish may last only a few minutes before he or she is whisked into the open ocean. Some divers overcome the time constraints of current diving by

During the day, a mushroom coral (above) retracts its tentacles into its limestone skeleton. At night, it reaches out to trap tiny plants and animals.

In an encounter Palauans call "getting slimed," jellyfish surround a scuba diver (right). These marine invertebrates, trapped in Jellyfish Lake for eons, long ago lost their need and ability to sting.

using a reef hook, a three-foot-long line with a hook at both ends. One hook attaches to a scuba vest and the other to a nook or cranny in the reef. The hook extends the dive, but in the process of setting, adjusting, and releasing it, a diver damages the fragile corals. Healthy coral gardens are found in many other areas of Palau, but at Blue Corner major areas of coral are now barren white patches of rock. This little corner of the world shows what can happen when underwater wonders are overwhelmed by people's desire to see them at any cost.

Among Palau's other attractions are 80 marine lakes. Jellyfish Lake, with its extraordinary jellyfish population, is the most visited. Like the others, it is dark green, has poor visibility, and is as warm as bathwater. Each day, jellyfish slowly follow the sun's path across the lake, soaking up sunlight for the life-supporting algae in their tissues. Because they haven't needed to protect themselves from predators, these jellyfish have lost the ability to sting. Their lake was sealed off from the open ocean eons ago, and jellyfish-eaters, such as turtles, were locked out. Without the threat of getting stung, today's underwater explorers can swim freely among yellow polka-dotted jellyfish shimmering harmlessly in the sun.

The Belize Barrier Reef

....

Underwater Wonders

Caught in the act of breathing, not
attacking a nearby arrow crab, a moray
eel exposes its razor-sharp fangs. With
its mouth agape, the eel forces water
over gills located in its throat.

The second largest barrier reef in the world rises from the seafloor off the coast of Belize. A diver's paradise, it is known for fascinating coral formations, myriad fish and invertebrates, and exceptional water clarity.

On the ocean side of this 160-mile-long reef is a popular tourist destination known as Lighthouse Reef. Here, crystal-clear waters fill the famous Blue Hole, a crater more than 1,000 feet across and just over 400 feet deep. At the surface, healthy coral formations rim this wonder within a wonder, but at a depth of 125 feet, neither corals nor fish can be found. Instead, a diver finds stalactites formed during the Ice Age, when the world sea level was much lower and the Blue Hole was a subterranean cavern. The hole formed when the cavern's roof collapsed.

To the south is Glover's Reef, surrounded by waters so clear that visibility even at night is quite good: The long shaft of a diver's torch can pierce the water to a distance of 15 feet. Because it is several miles from the mainland, this reef is not affected by silt and sediment runoff.

At Glover's, the arrival of a diver startles bright red cardinalfish swimming in open water, causing them to quickly dart into the darkness, where they can "see," like all other fish, without light. To do this, they rely on organs called lateral lines running along both sides of their bodies. A combination of sonar and radar, a lateral line senses vibrations and movements in the water, allowing a fish to detect predators and prey. It's also an early warning device. As a fish swims, it creates a sort of bow wake that bounces off solid objects. When another fish feels the wake, it moves to avoid a collision.

Glover's Reef is home to the Emerald Forest, a site named for magnificent elkhorn coral "trees" having trunks a foot in diameter and canopies more than ten feet high. Several kinds of exotic fish also live here, and at night, a camera-bearing diver can catch them asleep, tucked in against the reef, but still out in the open. Butterflyfish as colorful as backyard butterflies hover in the water. So do hogfish with piglike snouts, trumpetfish that look like two-foot-long musical instruments, and parrotfish, their beaklike mouths closed for the night.

Not all of the reef's creatures are lost in sleep, however. Manta rays and sharks prowl the darkness, seeking meals. Lobsters, crabs, shrimp, and nudibranchs (the beautiful slugs of the sea) search the reef for food and mates. A Nassau grouper gets its mouth "cleaned" by a tiny shrimp, which darts from side to side and from top to bottom to remove small parasites and dead flesh from the cooperative fish, its mouth frozen in a wide yawn. The shrimp gets a free meal, so to speak. Dr. Mary Wicksten, a marine biologist at Texas A&M University

Its sharp dorsal spine enables the colorful black durgon (above) to ward off hungry predators. It also helps to anchor the fish in reef hideouts.

During the Ice Age, huge caverns formed in the Belize Barrier Reef. The roof of one collapsed, creating the 412-foot-deep Blue Hole (opposite).

and a specialist in these so-called cleaning stations, says that fish seek out established stations on the reef because the activity is important for their health. Like several other reef fish, the Nassau grouper is remarkable for its ability to change sex as it gets older, increasing its chances for reproductive success when another grouper is met.

At a natural cut in Glover's Reef, where water surges during the changing of the tide, a diver can free-fall horizontally, whipped along by the strong current. But fish hover without obvious effort, their streamlined bodies designed by nature to keep them in place in such conditions. Jutting from the walls of the cut, like fingers on

a huge hand, are lavender tube sponges that eat by filtering tiny plants and animals from the sea. Soft coral sea fans, also filter feeders, bend in the breezelike underwater current that brings them a constant supply of food. The dominant life-form here is the hard coral, which is capable of withstanding the force of very strong wave action.

Where the current exits this canyon, it stirs up sand from the floor of a lagoon, reducing visibility. Somewhere near the bottom, turtles and manatees leisurely feed on sea grasses, while small coral heads form mini-reefs alive with tiny fish.

Across the lagoon is the Hol Chan Marine Reserve, a small area off Ambergris Cay where the tangled roots of a mangrove forest reach into the water. Even here, small fish dart among the roots, looking for meals or protection from predators.

Hol Chan, which is Maya for "the cut," was established in 1987. It encompasses all three habitats of the barrier reef ecosystem: reef, lagoon, and mangroves. Although separate, each area depends on the others. Marine scientist Jacque Carter, who has long studied Belize's fish, writes: "The mangroves are a feeding and breeding ground for reef fishes; they also trap silt and sediment runoff before it reaches the reef. The lagoon is...a feeding ground for many reef fishes, and the sea grasses...trap reef-smothering particles [keeping them] from reaching the living reef.... The reef itself acts as a barrier, protecting the lagoon, mangroves and shore areas from destructive wave action. If one area is damaged, the others are also affected—which is why it is important to protect the entire system, and not just the beautiful coral reef."

Hovering just below the sunlit surface, an Atlantic bottlenose dolphin (above) explores the waters off Belize. These intelligent and friendly animals swim all along the barrier reef, in deep or shallow water. Yellow tube sponges (opposite), among the simplest multicellular reef animals, suck in water through small holes on their exteriors. After specialized cells filter out food and oxygen, the sponges release the water through openings at the ends of their tubes.

The Galápagos Islands

··········

Underwater Wonders

Graceful sea lions perform an
underwater ballet for snorkelers and
scuba divers in Galápagos waters. These
playful animals often nip divers' fins and
"bite" exhaled air bubbles.

Rising from the Pacific 600 miles west of Ecuador are arid islands whose name, for obvious reasons, is a Spanish word for tortoises. Indeed, the Galápagos Islands are famous for tortoises weighing hundreds of pounds. What many people don't know, though, is that fascinating creatures also live in an undersea realm offshore.

Describing the contrast between the islands and their underwater bounty in a 1924 book, *Galapagos: World's End*, William Beebe wrote: "Hosts of sally-lightfoots (tidal crabs) were the most brilliant spots of colour above the water in the islands, putting to shame the dull, drab hues of the terrestrial organisms and hinting at the glories of colourful animal life beneath the surface of the sea."

Four currents converge in Galápagos waters: the Peru or Humboldt from the south, the Equatorial from the west, the North Equatorial, and the Panama. Fish and invertebrates from different oceans and habitats ride these currents and quickly make themselves at home along the rocky shores, on the sandy sea bottom, and in the mangrove forests of the Galápagos.

Among the most playful creatures here are the sea lions. Slicing through the water at dazzling speeds, they sometimes perform an underwater ballet of sorts, twisting, turning, stretching, and arching their sleek bodies amid clouds of plankton. A sea lion will swim just inches from a diver's mask as if approaching for a kiss, or it will nibble at a swim fin or embrace a diver with its flippers, all the while maintaining eye contact—a technique that requires incredible flexibility and agility.

A sea monster the size of a school bus also lives in Galápagos waters: the whale shark. Largest fish in the sea, it eats plankton and fish strained from the water by its wide mouth. Although encounters with it are rare here, encounters with other sharks are not. Six- to eight-foot-long hammerhead sharks, with heads shaped like sledgehammers, swim in schools of a hundred or more. White-tip, Galápagos, and bull sharks, most larger than a man, are seen by nearly every explorer who enters these waters. Getting pictures of them while diving is difficult, though, because a diver's bubbles seem to frighten them.

Among the more unlikely denizens of equatorial waters are Galápagos penguins. Only here and along the Pacific coast of South America do penguins live near the Equator. They ply these waters with great ease, chasing

fish and avoiding sharks. Out of water, they may be seen waddling about on the islands' volcanic rocks.

Another unique animal is the marine iguana, a ferret-size lizard whose distinctly reptilian features are adaptations for its life in the Galápagos: It uses its blunt snout to scrape algae from submerged rocks, its clawed feet to grip slippery rocks, its muscular body and tail to swim in strong tides, and its spines to defend against predators.

Although the archipelago holds many wonders, it does not have a coral reef. Instead, divers find dramatic volcanic rock formations beneath the sea. Some of them are bare; others are covered by red algae, orange encrusting sponges, orange cup corals, and bushes of black coral.

Holding on tight in the rough surf, the archipelago's prehistoric-looking marine iguana (left) easily bites off chunks of algae from submerged rocks.

Underwater adventurers have nothing to fear from the slow-moving whale shark (top), a huge fish that eats only plankton and small fish.

Tucked safely away in a miniature topside cave, a Sally Lightfoot crab (above) can escape detection by sharp-eyed seabirds looking for a meal.

One reason for the low number of reef-building corals is a weather phenomenon called El Niño. Periodically, El Niño brings an incursion of water that is poor in nutrients and unusually warm; these conditions are unfavorable for corals and plankton. El Niño also causes rainfall to increase, and large amounts of freshwater added to seawater are detrimental to coral growth.

Conversely, these seas hold a high number of fish— 300 species, of which 17 percent are endemic. Among them are the hieroglyphic hawkfish, a bottom-dweller that seems to have symbols etched on its body, and the red-lipped batfish, with fashion-model-red lips. Not surprisingly, the archipelago attracts many fishermen.

Although the area is protected by a 1986 presidential decree making it a Marine Resource Reserve, it is still the site of illegal fishing. Park rangers simply don't have the resources to patrol almost 30,000 square miles. Luckily, the conservation effort is strong, being led in part by the owner of live-aboard dive vessels, Herbert Frei, Jr., who says that a plan is in the works to provide fishermen with a livelihood, while not significantly affecting the underwater habitat.

Efforts are also under way to save the islands' terrestrial animals, especially the tortoises. Because their shells come in different sizes and shapes—domed, saddle-backed, or somewhere in between—these gentle giants formerly were thought to be members of several species. In fact, there is only one species, and it was almost wiped out by hunting and habitat destruction. Today, scientists at the Charles Darwin Research Station are working to protect and, in some cases, reintroduce the giant tortoises to more remote areas of the archipelago.

Fortunately, some 750,000 birds still can be found among the islands. Flycatchers, mockingbirds, yellow warblers, hawks, owls, and finches are common. So are 19 species of seabirds, including the blue-footed booby, red-footed booby, frigate bird, and the waved albatross.

When naturalist Charles Darwin first came to the Galápagos in 1835, he noticed that animals of the same species looked different on different islands. Years later, he developed a revolutionary theory of evolution and wrote *On the Origin of Species by Means of Natural Selection.* What might he have thought if he had also seen the remarkable creatures in the seas surrounding the islands?

Like a squadron of attacking enemy planes, several hammerhead sharks cruise over a rocky pinnacle. Scuba divers rarely get close to hammerheads because their bubbles frighten away the shy animals.

The Northern Red Sea

....

Underwater Wonders

Colorful soft corals, like this gorgonian photographed at night, draw divers from around the world to the warm waters of the northern Red Sea.

Surrounded by one of the world's largest expanses of sand, the Red Sea laps the shores of an ecosystem seemingly devoid of life. For that reason, many people find it difficult to imagine that some of the earth's richest coral reefs rise from the floor of the sea's northern reaches.

Marine scientist Eugenie Clark has no such difficulty: "If I could only dive in one place in the world, I would choose Râs Muhammad." Having researched life in the Red Sea for more than four decades, she believes this area best represents the Red Sea's many marine splendors. In 1980, Dr. Clark encouraged the Egyptian government to make the site a national park, an idea that became a reality in 1983.

A coral plateau in deep water, Râs Muhammad has sometimes been called an underwater Garden of Eden, a quiet place with the feel of a church. Shafts of sunlight illuminate the reef's red, yellow, orange, and light-green soft corals. Hard corals such as stars, fingers, and clubs are also found here, ensuring that the community is rock solid.

Some sea anemones on the reef seem to glow a brilliant shade of orange, a color that comes from algae in their tentacles. Although many photographers have tried, no one has yet been able to capture this glow on film. Now and then a diver will witness a very rare sight: bright-red lionfish swimming in open water during the day. Equipped with venomous dorsal spines, these fish usually reside near the sea bottom, waiting to trap smaller fish in nooks and crannies.

Several divers have met "George," a reef monster the size of a beanbag chair. A humphead wrasse, this fish has chameleon eyes, cowlike lips, and a body pattern in the form of an intricate green maze on a blue background. Although George is a strange-looking creature, he is, in fact, a friendly fish seeking only handouts from divers.

At Râs Muhammad some divers also have unforgettable encounters with the reef triggerfish. One moment

this foot-long fish may be blowing water into a small hole on a shallow ledge. The next instant it may be charging at full speed, its fangs bared. But two feet away, it will suddenly stop, like a flying saucer in a science-fiction movie, and retreat. The triggerfish repeats this charge several times. When it no longer feels threatened, it goes about its business, perhaps tending its nest of newly laid eggs.

Another popular reef, Anemone City, boasts vast numbers of anemones. This reef is a swaying shag carpet of white and green tentacles. Darting in and out among the tentacles are hundreds of clownfish, sporting upside-down smiles, and domino-fish, their black bodies dotted with white spots.

For the sport diver, Anemone City provides a great deal of entertainment. But for marine scientists and divers who are interested in the mysteries of the sea, it is a living laboratory and a stage for observing one of the most fascinating examples of symbiosis in the marine world—the relationship between clownfish and sea anemones. A clownfish, for its part, protects an anemone from fish that like to eat its soft tentacles. The anemone, in turn, offers a haven for the clownfish, which finds safety among tentacles whose stings, for some reason, don't hurt it.

Clownfish present marine scientists with another interesting aspect of life in the sea. These fish, like many other reef fish species, are hermaphrodites: They have both male and female sex organs, although not at the same time. Such attributes increase the chances of a species' survival. If a female clownfish is eaten or dies

Reef goldfish (opposite) find safety in numbers and in speed. At the sight of a predator, they dart lightning fast into the reef's nooks and crannies.

Once part of a thriving coral reef, now-barren blocks of fossilized corals (above) rise as rocky heights beside today's Red Sea. Just inches below the surface, marine life continues to thrive.

naturally, for example, the largest juvenile turns into a breeding female.

Adventurous divers can explore caves and caverns at a site known as Fishermen's Bank. Here in the darkness, large schools of hatchet-shaped glassy sweepers swim in tight formation, fluttering their tiny fins and making swishing sounds as they sweep around divers' bodies. Lionfish may swim near the ceilings of the caves, their venomous dorsal spines pointing downward toward divers' heads. In some caves, small openings in the ceiling are penetrated by dramatic shafts of light, an underwater show that frequently mesmerizes divers bold enough to swim here.

To learn why the Red Sea has such a diversity of species—1,000 species of tropical fish and 400 species of corals—scientists have had to go a long way back in time. Thirty million years ago, the Red Sea was closed at its southern end. Its northern end, however, opened into the Mediterranean Sea, allowing Atlantic species to enter and breed. About ten million years later, shifts in the earth's

Illuminated by a diver's flash, a massive school of longnose parrotfish (above) stands out against a coral reef. In natural light their coloration helps them blend into the scenery. A longnose hawkfish (opposite) rests among soft corals, waiting to pounce on shrimp or crabs that come crawling by.

tectonic plates closed the Red Sea's northern end and opened its southern one, letting in species from the Indian Ocean. The tectonic shifts had produced a sea with both Atlantic and Indo-Pacific species, although the latter now dominate.

Another reason for the diversity of marine life is the region's exceptionally clear skies. Intense sunlight provides abundant solar energy for the corals and the photo-synthesizing zooxanthellae that live inside them. The more sunlight corals get, the faster they grow. Healthy reef structures in the Red Sea have more places for fish to find food and hide from predators; hence, a healthier, more diverse fish population that is a wonder to behold.

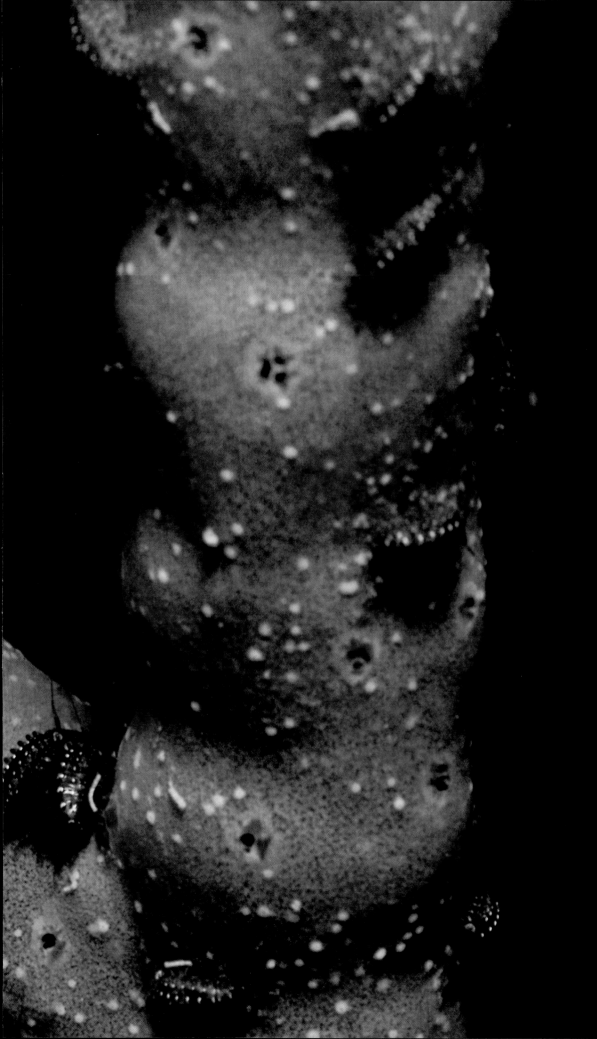

Lake Baikal

....

Underwater Wonders

Perched on a sponge colored green by its resident algae, a sculpin spies a possible meal. Slow-moving bottom-dwellers, sculpins comprise 80 percent of Lake Baikal's fish biomass.

In early March, snow still blankets Lake Baikal, its deep waters sealed beneath three-foot-thick ice. Over the next two months, under a bright springtime sun, the ice will slowly thaw in a process punctuated by cracking sounds not unlike the sharp report of guns. As long as the ice remains in place, though, scientists can set up camp right in the middle of this 400-mile-long, 5,000-foot-deep lake.

Russia's "Sacred Lake" is 25 million years old—the oldest lake on the planet. It is also the deepest lake, holding more water than all of North America's Great Lakes combined. Its aquatic life comprises more than 1,500 animal species and 1,000 plant species, two-thirds of which are endemic. According to marine scientist Andy Rechnitzer, Baikal is more biologically diverse than other lakes because oxygen-rich water circulates from its surface to its deepest depths, a process likely related to geothermal vents.

One of the most interesting animals in the lake is the Baikal seal, or nurpa, the world's only freshwater seal. Nurpas use their sharp claws to carve dens for their families while ice is still forming. Finding their dens is relatively easy: Look for air bubbles trapped in the ice after being exhaled by nurpas. You can also look for small breathing holes poked into snowdrifts by the seals.

Sharp spines on its back help protect an amphipod (opposite, upper) from crustacean-eating fish that live in Lake Baikal. Overcast skies can warn of a sudden 80-mph tempest called a sarma. Seasoned lake explorers seek refuge on shore (opposite, lower) when clouds roll in and the wind rises.

Tethered to a research ship, this remotely operated vehicle (above) helped National Geographic's Emory Kristof safely explore Baikal's bone-chilling depths.

For a diver to get into a den is another story. First, a diving crew member must use a metal saw to cut a small hole in the ice. Then a circular, manhole-size opening is cut with a chain saw, and long poles are used to push the round slab under the ice. To keep the hole from freezing over, it must be constantly raked. A team effort, indeed. Under the ice, the water is warmer than the air (36°F), but it is still very cold for scuba diving. Every 30 seconds or so, divers must tug on safety lines attached to their wrists to let the crew above know that they are all right.

Seen from an underwater perspective, the seal's den is an intricate ice carving, complete with tunnels and an igloo-like canopy that functions as an air pocket. Nurpas are shy, and pups resting on a bunk bed of ice quickly dive into the water when startled by a visitor.

In June, conditions at Lake Baikal are much different. Although the water temperature is about the same as it is in spring, the air temperature is usually in the 60s. Visibility underwater is perhaps 200 feet, many times greater than that in most lakes. The "great vis" at that time of year is caused by the water's relative lack of minerals and by countless small crustaceans eating the algae, plankton, and bacteria that can cloud freshwater and saltwater alike. Clarity does not last long, however. By mid-July, an algae bloom produces pea-soup conditions.

Except for the numbing cold that pains their ears, face, and fingers within minutes of entering the water, divers exploring the shallows of Baikal might feel as if they are hovering over a meadow on a sunny day. Looking up from a depth of 50 feet, they can see clouds in the sky. Looking down, they see fields of fluffy green algae.

The green spires of three-foot-tall candelabra sponges poke through the algae. Such large sponges, which get their color from algae living symbiotically in their tissues, are not rare in saltwater, but in other freshwater lakes they have no parallel. The sponges are homes for amphipods, alien-looking shrimplike creatures that are as small as specks or as large as human thumbs. And the waters of Lake Baikal hold 240 species of them.

Hiding among the sponges and algae are sculpins, bottom-dwelling fish that are masters of camouflage, their patterned bodies blending in with their surroundings. These ancient fish, like most cold-water species, don't move fast; it's just too cold here to make quick moves. So, the lake's 40 species of sculpins, comprising 80 percent of Baikal's fish biomass, rely on camouflage for protection against larger fish.

Near the lake's northern end, at a depth of approximately 1,350 feet, a geothermal vent provides warmth for a community of sponges, snails, worms, and fish living in a pitch-dark environment. The existence of this vent confirms that Baikal is a place where continental masses are being pulled apart. Photographer Emory Kristof, who has

Baikal seals, like this young pup just leaving its icy den (above), can descend to depths of 500 feet to find food. The dark circle at lower right forms the den's underwater entrance. A ship (opposite) carries passengers and cargo to Listvyanka, one of the few lakeside towns accessible by water in winter.

visited the site for the National Geographic Society, explains: "The communities of life resemble organisms normally found in an ocean, which gives weight to the theory that Baikal is an ocean in the making."

One rarely seen creature is the omul, a delicious fish endemic to the lake. Its scarcity indicates Baikal is ecologically out of balance, a result of the destructive effects of industrial development and logging nearby. Vadim Fialkov, of the Lake Baikal Limnological Institute, reports that "local environmental groups have put pressure on the government to reduce the amount of effluents that are dumped into the lake. With some luck, we'll get Baikal back to its pristine state and keep it that way." To help the effort, UNESCO has recommended that the lake and its watershed be designated a World Heritage Site.

Underwater Wonders
....

The Great Barrier Reef

....

Underwater Wonders

Blue chromis hide from predators in a dense forest of hard coral branches. Seldom straying far from home, these small fish snap up plankton floating in the ocean current.

The massive limestone pinnacle, six or seven stories high, is bathed in the soft light of early morning. From a distance, all looks tranquil, but up close, attackers can be seen everywhere. A crown-of-thorns sea star strafes the surface of hard corals. An octopus, in camouflage, wrestles a moray eel. A sea anemone, spreading its tentacles, snares an unsuspecting fish. Hawkfish are on the lookout, their eagle eyes searching the terrain for weaker fish. A small shrimp digs a hideout, while a goby fights off shrimp predators. A hundred or more convict tangs pick at healthy patches of algae essential to the reef's survival.

For thousands of years, such life-or-death struggles have been unfolding here at Pixie Pinnacle. And for just as long, life's sweeter moments have been playing out as well: Butterflyfish, paired for life, dance along the reef. Tomato clownfish play among sea anemones' tentacles. A damselfish farms algae early in the morning. Coral polyps, their rings of tentacles extended, soak up bright sunlight, nourishing the algae that live in their bodies. And lobsters, their antennae constantly twitching, play hide-and-seek with predators and prey alike.

Darting around the tentacles of a mushroom coral, cleaner shrimp (left) wait for "clients." When a fish approaches, the shrimp hop on and remove small parasites and dead flesh.

Saddle-back clownfish (above), like other members of their species, develop both male and female organs—although not at the same time—thus providing a greater chance of reproductive success and survival.

This coral pinnacle on the Great Barrier Reef holds many wonders. Yet it is only one of the countless biologically diverse sites on the enormous reef stretching 1,250 miles along Australia's northeast coast.

The longest barrier reef in the world has been called the "world's largest living creature." But it is neither a

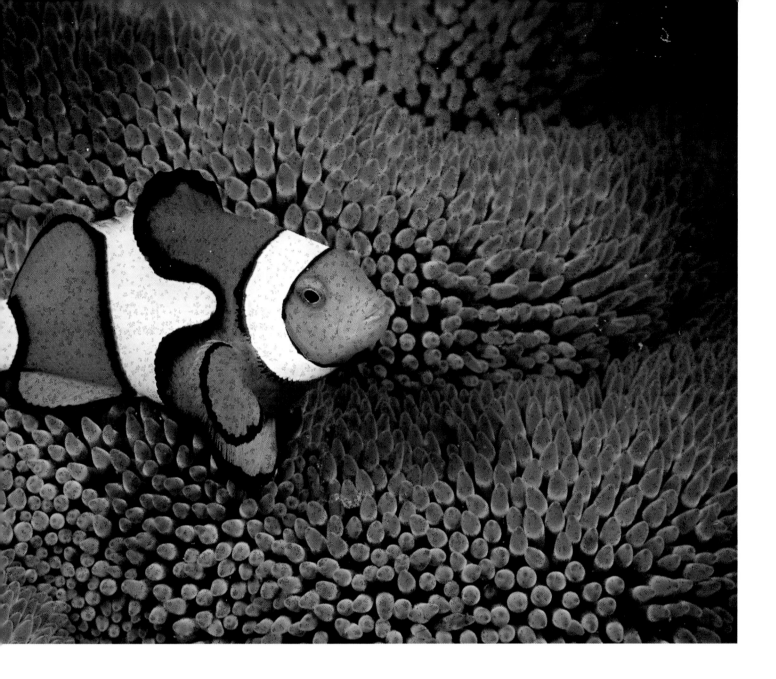

continuous reef nor a single, interconnected structure or organism. It is, in fact, a complex of more than 2,900 submerged coral reefs and some 900 coral and continental islands, an awe-inspiring wonder encompassing about 135,000 square miles of ocean and hosting 1,500 species of fish and 400 species of corals.

A true barrier reef includes a reef, its adjacent lagoon area, and mangrove thickets. Ribbon reefs at the northern end of the complex function as barrier reefs, protecting the mainland from strong ocean currents and trade winds. They look like long, flowing ribbons when seen by passengers aboard high-flying airplanes.

Along with pretty clownfish, angelfish, butterflyfish, and wrasses, an unusually high number of poisonous animals can be found in this area of the reef. Contact with such animals as box jellyfish, sea snakes, cone-shells, and blue-ringed octopuses can result in death if the victim is not treated immediately and properly. Scientists say, though, that some of these creatures hold substances found to be effective in the treatment of human illness.

Some sea creatures—hard corals—hold the key to the continued growth and development of the reef itself. Once a year, in late spring, the Great Barrier Reef is the scene of an extraordinary event: mass coral spawning. During the same few nights, more than a hundred hard coral species release millions of eggs and sperm, creating an underwater "snowstorm." After fertilization, the embryos float away to form new coral communities.

Farther south, relatively calm waters cover the wider part of Australia's continental shelf. Here, the reef's

Seemingly lost in a school of fusiliers, a thin batfish (opposite) turns sideways at the sight of a potential predator, creating the illusion of a large body. Sheltered from strong wave action beyond the reef, dive boats (above) show underwater explorers some of the wonders of the Great Barrier Reef.

marine life is not as abundant as it is in northern areas, but it is more accessible and a major attraction for scuba divers, who may encounter one of the reef's six species of marine turtles. Coral life still thrives, and so does one well-known fish species—the great white shark, which seems to prefer the cooler waters.

The Great Barrier Reef illustrates how conservation, when managed effectively, can satisfy the different interests of environmentalists, scientists, tourists, and fishermen. The plan for the reef was originally developed in 1975, when the Australian Parliament named the entire reef a national park and established the Great Barrier Reef Marine Park Authority (GBRMPA). The plan sets aside certain areas for tourism, sportfishing, and commercial fishing, and it limits access to other areas. About

one percent of the Great Barrier Reef is off-limits except for scientific research.

According to scientists at the Australian Institute of Marine Science (AIMS), some areas of the reef's northern section are badly damaged. But blame for the destruction can be borne only in part by careless divers. Much of the damage appears to have been caused by tropical storms, which in recent years have increased in number, perhaps because of global warming.

The crown-of-thorns sea star is also blamed for the poor conditions of some reefs. Scientists at GBRMPA say that increases in this coral-eater's population during the 1960s and 1980s decimated large areas. The problem was compounded, however, by efforts to destroy the animal. Fishermen and tour operators caught large numbers of sea stars, cut them up, and tossed them back into the ocean, not knowing that just a small piece of body attached to an arm can regenerate an entire animal.

Fortunately, through the efforts of GBRMPA and AIMS, word is spreading that protection and management of the Great Barrier Reef are essential for future research, exploration, and tourism.

The Deep-Sea Vents

....

Underwater Wonders

Powerful lights on *Mir I*, a manned submersible, illuminate a cluster of mineral
chimneys at a deep-sea vent site. Two
and a half miles below the surface of
the Atlantic, tiny white shrimp feed on
bacteria in superheated water.

In the blackness of night, on a remote part of the planet, a volcano erupts. Thick plumes of what looks like black smoke billow from it. Escaping magma blankets the terrain; temperatures soar to more than 600°F. Deep cracks form around the volcano, and superheated water seeps from them.

Local residents do not evacuate the area. While the magma is fatal to them, the hot water is not, and thousands are able to thrive in a seemingly hellish habitat.

The violent eruption, which has been going on for weeks, is not typical volcanic activity. It is happening at a deep-sea vent more than 8,000 feet below the surface of the ocean.

Deep-sea vents are also known as deepwater seeps, deep-sea springs, and hydrothermal vents. Found at the bottom of the ocean, they are created by volcanic and tectonic activity in areas where huge crustal plates are converging or spreading apart. Magma erupts along the margins of these plates, usually slowly, but sometimes with such ferocity that it creates instant lava lakes. The thick black smoke is actually a plume of metal-rich, superheated water billowing out of a silt- and sediment-covered, gray-and-black chimney—an underwater volcano.

Under thousands of pounds of pressure per square inch, seawater gradually seeps into the vents, where it is superheated and filled with manganese and other minerals before it is eventually returned to the ocean. This discovery has led some scientists to speculate that each drop of seawater circulates through the earth's crust, by way of the vents, every 10 to 20 million years. Before the discovery of the vents, most scientists thought that all of the minerals in the sea were dropped into the ocean by continental rivers.

Because no sunlight reaches the depths where the vents are found, these underwater wonders are visible only in the floodlights of a manned submersible such as

Hoisted with great care after hours on the seafloor, *Alvin,* a manned submersible (left), returns to its mother ship, the *Atlantis II* research vessel.

Entangled in a deepwater embrace, two male octopuses of different species (below) exhibit a form of mating behavior—a first-time observation in the wild.

Dancing over a field of tube worms, a blind crab (opposite) searches for its next meal near water heated to temperatures that exceed 600°F.

Alvin. This three-person submarine, which can descend 12,800 feet below sea level, first took photographers and research scientists to see vents along the Galápagos Rift in 1977, when the original discovery was made.

The residents of the vent community, although surely not the prettiest creatures, are perhaps the most fascinating of all the world's underwater wonders from a scientific perspective. At the geothermal vents, marine biologists have an opportunity to study a food chain that functions without sunlight. Most biologists had once believed that only sunlight, through photosynthesis, could support life on earth. At the vents, however, life begins with bacteria that metabolize hydrogen sulfide. The bacteria, in turn, become food for the other animals in the vent community.

Among the 300 species of life found near the vents, perhaps the best-documented life-forms are the giant red-tipped tube worms—12-foot-tall creatures whose 300,000 tentacles strain food from the water. By comparison, tube worms in the shallow ocean have a dozen or so tentacles and grow only a few inches long.

Blind crabs and shrimp, which don't need to see in a lightless world, live among octopuses that eat crabs and mussels. Equally fascinating residents include pink vent-fish, sea cucumbers, sponges, and brittle stars, flowerlike animals that use their fine appendages to anchor themselves to rocks.

Mussels are among the 48 documented species of mollusks found in vent communities. And some specimens of giant clams that live in this environment measure almost ten inches in length.

How does a vent become colonized? Some species, while in their larval stage, travel tremendous distances through a virtually lifeless and totally lightless realm to colonize a new vent on the seafloor. But other species first travel to the surface to feed before settling down at a new deep-sea vent.

Several of these vents have been found and explored in both the Pacific and the Atlantic, while others likely remain hidden a mile or more below the sea surface and await discovery. Scientists who study the life-forms near the vents believe that the bacteria there, as insignificant as they may seem to most people, may provide clues to how life first formed on this planet so many millions of years ago.

Vent communities hold thriving populations of giant tube worms, blind crabs, and strange-looking creatures like this pale, eel-like fish. Marine scientists have found more than 300 new species at such sites.

To imagine the magnificence of the world's seven ancient wonders—all but one of which are lost forever—we must rely on accounts that were written or handed down by eyewitnesses and their near contemporaries. That list of wonders, in all likelihood, is fixed forever unless archaeologists make a discovery of monumental proportions.

In the natural world (including the underwater realm) most of the wonders are eons-old works in progress. That list of superlatives also is unlikely to change in our time—unless another volcano pops up as Mexico's Paricutín did in 1943. Natural wonders develop according to nature's schedule.

Compared with the other splendors, the wonders of the modern world represent a plethora of possibilities. In the 20th century, spectacular advances in design, engineering, and construction yielded an array of monumental structures. And from these, the American Society of Civil Engineers (ASCE), with help from experts around the world, selected these wonders: the Empire State Building, the Itaipú Dam, the CN Tower, the Panama Canal, the Channel Tunnel, the North Sea Protection Works, and the Golden Gate Bridge.

While cultural wonders of the distant past often served the lofty ideals of love, the divine, and the afterlife, the modern world's wonders exemplify pragmatism. They were designed to meet the needs of commerce, to improve transportation and communications systems, to produce energy, and, in one case, to save a country from the sea. Embodying an abundance of human ingenuity, they showcase humankind's ability to dream, plan, and achieve on a colossal, mind-boggling scale. Other, more modern, wonders may eventually supplant the list offered here, but they undoubtedly will continue to fulfill the ASCE's charge, serving as "a tribute to universal human desire to triumph over the impossible."

SEVEN WONDERS of the MODERN WORLD

· · · · · · · · · ·

by Catherine Herbert Howe

Rising against the San Francisco skyline the south tower of the Golden Gate Bridge reaches 746 feet. With its northern companion, it remains the world's tallest suspension bridge tower.

The Empire State Building

··········

Modern Wonders

Sunlight bathes the Empire State
Building while its midtown Manhattan
neighbors wait in shadow. Icon of 1930s
sleekness, the tower topped all other
skyscrapers for more than 40 years.

Air of nonchalance belies the dangers of a steel-working team's labor (above). The pair guides a beam into position for riveting. With the Hudson River as backdrop (opposite), a worker performs high-wire artistry to fasten a cable. Fourteen men died during the Empire State Building's construction.

Anything was possible in the glorious 1920s, especially in New York, the city that never slept. New and modern concepts were embraced, not feared. Each week, it seemed, some record-breaking feat was accomplished; size and power ruled. The time was ripe for a building to assume center stage, to outreach every other skyscraper, and to transform, irrevocably, the Manhattan skyline.

A symbol of hope to all New Yorkers—even after the Depression intervened—the Empire State Building started to rise on St. Patrick's Day in 1930. And with a precision and timeliness that belied the pathbreaking nature of its height and design, it was finished an astonishing 14 months later, in May 1931.

The driving force behind the project was former New York governor and failed presidential candidate Al Smith. In 1929, newly "retired" from 40 years of public service, he persuaded developers and financiers to support construction of an office building surpassing all other New York landmarks in height and splendor. Despite the tenuous financial climate, Smith garnered both the enthusiasm and funding to make the project possible.

The Smith-headed Empire State Building Corporation purchased a well-known property for its megaproject. Covering nearly two acres on Fifth Avenue between 33rd and 34th Streets, the Waldorf-Astoria Hotel had passed its heyday as a fashionable hostelry and showplace for New York's elite. When the first buyer defaulted on payments, Smith arranged the purchase through his consortium.

For architects the corporation chose Shreve, Lamb & Harmon, a local firm known for solid, conventionally modern office buildings and uncompromisable ethics. For contractors they chose Starrett Bros. & Eken, a firm that had collaborated with the century's finest architects and which had a reputation for speed.

Legend has it that John J. Raskob, who played money man to Al Smith's politicking front man, held up a humble pencil when asked what the colossal office building

Modern Wonders
··········

Rays of the sun emanate from a mural (above) in the Empire State Building's three-story lobby. The mural, in marble and aluminum, depicts the seven classical wonders, adding its host as the eighth. Sightseers appear as ants on the building's outdoor observation deck, 86 floors high (opposite).

knew they had to finish in time to meet the traditional commercial leasing date—May 1—the following year.

What happened next boggles the mind. Without the aid of computers, the contractors drew up exhaustive lists and schedules for building materials. (It helped that the building design did not call for elaborate ornamentation and handwork and that the main components could be produced in bulk.) They chose suppliers who could meet their tight deadlines for Indiana limestone and granite; Pittsburgh steel; New York cement; Italian, English, and German marble; northern lumber; and myriad other products. Steel traveled directly to a supply yard in New Jersey, where it was numbered for floor and position and sent two floors at a time to the job site. Relentless supervision and anticipation of detail became the hallmark of the building's designers, contractors, and engineers.

The Empire State Building rose on 210 massive steel box columns extending from the foundation to the 86th floor. Derricks lifted beams and other materials to each floor, where they were rolled to their positions by a small-gauge railway. Riveting teams plied their daredevil trade high above the city, often securing beams made just three days before in a Pennsylvania factory.

Construction of the tower and mast brought the building to its final height. With interior finishing, including the 67 Otis elevators that made the structure capable of occupancy, the completed project cost 41 million dollars, a modest amount by today's standards. Part of that price tag covered some 10 million bricks, 70 miles of water pipes, and 17 million feet of telephone wire.

From the time of the project's conception, publicists worked tirelessly to promote what they dubbed "The Eighth Wonder of the World." No stunt was too outlandish and no tie-in too far-fetched to be considered by the relentless hawkers. Before the building was officially opened, publicists had exploited the ill-fated attempts to use the mast for blimp-mooring. Opening day itself was a carnival of events presided over by Al Smith in his trademark brown derby. In the decades that followed, numerous celebrities, including television's Lassie and Mount Everest's Sir Edmund Hillary, were whisked to the top to pose for pictures. In times of joy or sorrow, the Empire State Building mirrored the city's emotions, its decorative lights all aglow or temporarily dimmed.

Although the 1972 completion of the first of the World Trade Towers—"shoeboxes standing on end," according to one critic—usurped the Empire State Building's claim for height, it did not diminish the building's position as New York's most cherished icon. Nearly 70 years after its completion, the Empire State Building remains "architecturally excellent from top to bottom."

would look like. Before getting final approval, however, architect William F. Lamb would present 16 versions of the design. The originally planned 85-story building grew to 102 floors reaching a height of 1,250 feet. A "mooring mast," designed as a docking point for dirigibles, brought the total to 1,454 feet. At that height, the Empire State Building would easily outreach its nearest rival, the 1,048-foot Chrysler Building.

Excavation of the site began even before the walls of the Waldorf-Astoria were totally removed. And although Manhattan schist, the bedrock anchoring most of the island, appeared only 35 feet down, 28,500 truckloads of earth, rock, and other debris already had been hauled away. By then it was mid-March 1930, and the builders

The Itaipú Dam

··········

Modern Wonders

Great clouds of water and mist rage through the spillway of the Itaipú Dam. The tremendous force of 16 million gallons of water may erupt into the spillway every second.

You hear it long before you can see it. Somewhere past the curtain of a thick mountain forest, waters of the Paraná River explode through a massive, 400-yard-wide spillway at more than 90 miles an hour. The roar is deafening. Behind the dam, other waters rush into penstocks, or water tubes, and over turbines that charge 18 mammoth generators. This system of the Itaipú Dam, running at full tilt, transforms the force of the water into 12,600 megawatts of electricity, enough to meet all of the power needs of Paraguay and one-third of the needs of Brazil, two countries that share the Paraná River as a border. Put another way, the Itaipú Dam, at any one time, can produce enough electricity to almost completely power the state of California.

One of the most ambitious hydroelectric projects in the world, the Itaipú Dam was a product of the economic boom time enjoyed by Brazil in the 1970s. Although a bilateral agreement in 1973 made its neighbor Paraguay an equal partner and owner of half the power that would be generated, Brazil alone obtained funding for the project. This apparent altruism stemmed from the much-larger country's hopes that electricity produced at home would eventually reduce its dependence on imported petroleum by saving more than half a million barrels of oil per day. Brazil also hoped that the local power source would fuel industrial productivity in the southeastern part of the country. From the beginning, the economic arrangement called for Paraguay to sell its surplus power to Brazil.

The Itaipú project is actually the last of a series of dams controlling the flow of the Paraná, the second longest river system in South America, after the Amazon. The Itaipú Dam turns the river into an enormous reservoir covering almost 520 square miles. Reaching about one hundred miles upstream, the reservoir flooded the once awesome Guaíra Falls, which—until that time—had been the world's greatest falls in terms of water volume.

The first step in this colossal undertaking undid millions of years of work by natural forces. To allow construction of the main dam in the natural riverbed, workers rerouted part of the Paraná into a new, man-made channel. In 1975, on the river's left bank, or

Concrete and steel in Itaipú's unfinished powerhouse stretch across the channel of the Paraná River. The completed plant houses 18 generators expected to produce a trillion kilowatt-hours by the year 2002.

Workers adjust a thyristor convertor valve in a converter station (right) seven miles from the dam. Each four-story valve structure converts alternating current to direct current or vice versa. The Itaipú Dam (opposite) extends five miles across the border shared by Paraguay and Brazil, the two countries that benefit from its electrical output.

Brazilian side, workers began removing 56.4 million tons of rock to fashion a parallel diversion channel 1.3 miles long, 500 feet wide, and 300 feet deep. At the same time, other workers were erecting cofferdams at the new channel's entrance and exit, all preparatory to the building of the control dam, 12 sluices, and part of the powerhouse in the diversion channel.

In 1978, a powerful blast of dynamite destroyed the cofferdams and sent water coursing for the first time through the diversion channel. With that crucial component now operational, workers raced against the coming of the flood season. New cofferdams had to be built, closing off the river's flow in the area of the natural channel where the main dam would be constructed. Temporary structures, the upstream and downstream cofferdams each measured 1,800 feet long and 295 feet tall. With cofferdams complete, the work site was pumped dry.

All the energy of a peak 40,000-man workforce poured into the construction of the main dam and its enormous powerhouse. Six on-site concrete plants constantly churned out the chief building material, using ice instead of water—a key ingredient—in the warm climate. By substituting ice, they could control the temperature during the setting process and thus keep the concrete from cracking.

Even though Itaipú's main dam boasted a concrete-sparing hollow design, more than 30 million metric tons of concrete—enough to build 400 miles of a six-lane highway—were still needed to complete the project. In all, this project consumed five times more concrete than Hoover Dam, which the United States built in 1936.

As the main dam wall rose to a height of 643 feet, the powerhouse began to take shape. Imagine a factory that is the size of a half-mile-long cathedral, half-submerged in the waters of a mighty river. Inside the powerhouse are 18 generators measuring 52 feet in diameter and standing 7 stories tall, each one taking the water from a 466-foot-long penstock into its turbines. A curved and

concrete-buttressed wing dam connects the main dam to the quarter-mile-long spillway, designed to handle any amount of overflow the pent-up Paraná can unleash. The rest of Itaipú's nearly five-mile length is composed of earth- or rock-fill embankment dams that stretch out on both sides of the reservoir.

Following the completion of the main dam in the river's natural channel, sluice gates in the control dam cut off the water supply to the diversion channel. Over 14 days and nights in October 1982, the water rose more than 300 feet in a deluge of biblical proportions, backing up in a reservoir behind the main dam. Once the water reached the crest of the spillway, the river's flow was returned to the natural bed. The cofferdam in the downstream side of the control dam was reconstructed, and

the sluice gates were concreted over. Since then, the river's overflow has gushed through the spillway to the right of the main dam. At times, the spillway handles a discharge of 16 million gallons per second. Two more years passed before Itaipú's first generator went on-line; 7 more passed before all 18 generators assumed their duties in commercial power production.

By the time the project was completed, its cost had reached a staggering 12 billion dollars. But the dam has had more than an economic impact on the region: Nearly 400 square miles are considered protected areas where water quality, fisheries, and forests are closely monitored.

Today, few sights are as breathtaking as a visitor's first glimpse of the Itaipú complex, standing "like a concrete temple high above the Paraná River."

The CN Tower

....

Modern Wonders

Toronto's crowning glory, the
CN Tower rises 1,815.5 feet above
western Lake Ontario. Built to improve
communications in a growing city, the
tower boasts many superlatives.

It is fitting that television, the technological wonder that profoundly changed life in the 20th century, spurred the building of the era's tallest freestanding structure. In the late 1960s, Toronto's soaring skyline began to play havoc with signals from conventional transmission towers. Signals bouncing off the city's skyscrapers produced a number of problems, including the annoying phenomenon of "ghosting" on television sets. Weaker signals competed with stronger ones, giving viewers the effect of watching two programs at once. To improve the situation, Canadian National Railways, or CN, proposed building a transmission tower that would stand head and shoulders—and then some—above Toronto's tallest buildings.

A Toronto firm prepared the initial design, enlisting the aid of engineering experts the world over. Their original plan showed three towers linked by structural bridges. Gradually the design evolved into a single 1,815.5-foot-tall tower comprised of three hollow "legs."

Foundation work began in 1973. Giant backhoes excavated more than 62,000 tons of earth and shale to a depth of 50 feet from a site along the shore of Lake Ontario in Toronto Harbor. Next, prestressed concrete and reinforced steel were arranged in a Y-shaped pattern 22 feet thick. Each hollow leg of the Y would carry its fair share of the tower's 130,000-ton burden.

The foundation took only four months to complete. The tower itself presented a challenge of height never before met by the technique of poured concrete. To meet that challenge, engineers designed a huge mold known as a slip form. Concrete was poured 24 hours a day, five days a week, and as it hardened, the mold moved upward by means of a ring of hydraulic jacks. The ascending slip form gradually decreased in girth to give the tower its tapering shape. In the words of one science editor, "the tower wasn't so much built as it was extruded."

When the tower reached the 1,100-foot mark, the builders made preparations for the SkyPod, a seven-story structure housing two observation decks, a revolving restaurant, a nightclub, and broadcasting equipment. The SkyPod is anchored by 12 steel-and-wooden brackets that were slowly pushed up the tower by 45 hydraulic jacks. Concrete formed the SkyPod's "walls," and a doughnut-shaped ring, called a radome, was added to its base to protect the delicate microwave dishes receiving radio and television transmissions. The SkyPod is reached by four high-speed, glass-fronted elevators whose rapid rise simulates a jetliner's takeoff, unless weather conditions call for a much slower ascent.

The concrete tower continues above the SkyPod, ending at the Space Deck 1,465 feet up. The Space Deck receives support from cantilevers extending out of the concrete section beneath it. After a 58-second elevator ride from the SkyPod below, visitors can enjoy breathtaking vistas from a glass-enclosed balcony. On a clear day they might be able to glimpse sites 75 miles away.

For the last phase of construction, a Sikorsky Skycrane helicopter arrived to install the tower's 335-foot communications mast. One by one the helicopter lifted about 40 seven-ton sections of the mast to the top of the tower, where workers braved blustery March winds to receive them. When the sections were in place, they were secured by a total of 40,000 bolts. Afterward, the entire mast was covered by a fiberglass-reinforced sheathing to prevent icing.

Of interest to Torontonians since construction began, the CN Tower gained additional fans with the arrival of the helicopter. Nicknamed Olga, its daily schedule was printed in newspapers, and changes were announced as breaking news on radio and television. With Olga, the mast assembly took a little longer than three weeks; without Olga, the job would have lasted six months.

Completed in 1975, the tower had cost 57 million dollars to build, a bargain compared with other modern wonders. It also boasted incredible statistics of precision and safety. During construction, surveyors' transits up to a thousand feet away focused on optical plumbs mounted on the slip-form base. The constant surveillance kept the structure an incredible 1.1 inches within plumb.

Engineers established a wind-tolerance standard for the tower of 260 miles an hour, a level well above nature's most extreme demands. Counterweights on the antenna correct for wobble in high winds. Because the tower is an easy target for lightning, copper grounding wires were installed. As a result, visitors can safely view some 75 spectacular strikes a year.

The CN Tower is a work in progress. In recent years the tower gained two new elevators to accommodate an increase in visitors. To accomplish this, the 2,579-step metal staircase was moved to the interior of the structure. In addition, a glass floor was added to the SkyPod's observation deck. Brave visitors, the majority not surprisingly children, inch out over the visual void. More often than not the experience is pronounced, "Awesome!"

Almost twice as tall as the Eiffel Tower and more than three times the height of the Washington Monument, the CN Tower has taken proud ownership of Toronto's skyline, while exorcising the ghosts from its TV sets.

Named the World's Tallest Building and Freestanding Structure by the *Guinness Book of World Records*, Toronto's CN Tower offers 75-mile panoramas.

The Panama Canal

· · · · · · · · · ·

Modern Wonders

Modern ships cruise through a stretch
of the Panama Canal. The 51-mile-long
waterway, completed in 1914, joined
Atlantic and Pacific, fulfilling its slogan,
"The Land Divided, the World United."

Little fanfare accompanied the SS *Ancon* when it steamed into the Panama Canal from the Atlantic Ocean on August 15, 1914. Only days before, war had broken out in Europe, adding anxiety and distraction to an event marking the end of four decades of monumental labor, incredible hardship, and repeated setbacks. But at the end of this day, after just a 51-mile journey lasting fewer than 10 hours, the *Ancon* celebrated its safe arrival at the Pacific coast. The nature of ship travel between the Atlantic and Pacific had changed forever.

Before the opening of the canal, a trip between New York and San Francisco meant either an arduous overland journey or a treacherous voyage around South America's gale-swept Cape Horn. The voyage took about one month and covered 13,000 miles. There had to be a better way, and for many people the place to look was Panama: A canal there would cut weeks as well as 8,000 miles from the ordeal.

The French were the first to try cutting across the isthmus. In 1880, Ferdinand de Lesseps tried to repeat the same kind of success he'd had in building the Suez Canal. But his plan for a sea level canal at Panama required an inordinate amount of digging and was undermined by the health hazards of working in a tropical climate. It had not yet been discovered that mosquitoes were the vectors for two lethal diseases, malaria and yellow fever. After 20 years and 20,000 deaths, the French effort came to an end.

The United States took on the project with the enthusiastic backing of President Theodore Roosevelt. In 1903, the U. S. had supported the Panamanians in a bid for independence from Colombia, to whom the French had paid a large fee for the right to build their canal. In 1904, an agreement with an independent Panama in hand, the U. S. began its work in the Canal Zone.

Army doctor Col. William C. Gorgas, who had successfully controlled yellow fever in Cuba, was called to Panama to wage war on the *Anopheles* and *Aedes* mosquitoes. He used nets, screens, sprays, and a thorough search-and-destroy tactic against possible breeding sites. This campaign lasted through the canal construction era.

It was clear to John F. Stevens, the project's newly appointed chief engineer, that the establishment of an efficient infrastructure would have to precede serious excavation. A railway builder by experience, Stevens reorganized the Panama Railroad. He also oversaw the building of new roads, construction camps, docks, and warehouses; the creation of water and sewage systems; and the preparation of meals for thousands of workers. In addition, the chief engineer lobbied members of the U. S. Congress and won their approval for a lock canal that would begin and end at sea level.

By 1907, however, an exhausted Stevens had written to the President, complaining about the pressure of the job and hinting at needing a rest. Roosevelt responded by cabling back acceptance of Stevens's "resignation." He then appointed Army Corps of Engineers Lt. Col. George Washington Goethals to the top position, and under his

Cement falls from a hopper during the construction of the massive Gatun Locks (opposite). The entire canal consumed more than 2.25 million barrels of concrete.

A mighty Bucyrus steam shovel moves tons of earth and rock with one chomp of its giant dipper (above). Shovels ran along one railroad track while they dumped their loads into spoil cars on another track.

The humble tug *Gatun* (left) runs a test transit of the locks of the same name in September 1913. The locks lifted the tug 85 feet from sea level to the elevation of Gatun Lake.

command, work proceeded on the canal. To complete the project, the labor force would eventually total 75,000.

The initial 7 miles of the canal involved excavation of a ship channel at least 38 feet deep. Where the terrain began to ascend, the first of three sets of locks was built. The set at Gatun required the installation of three pairs of locks—concrete chambers 1,000 feet long and 110 feet wide—to raise ships to an elevation of 85 feet. The locks have hollow steel gates, 65 feet wide and 7 feet thick, that close to a flattened V after a ship enters.

Workers dumped spoil across the capricious Chagres River to make the Gatun Dam. The dam turned the river into the 165-square-mile lake that would, at the turn of a handle, fill or empty a lock by means of 70 holes in the bottom of the chamber. The lake's spillway also produces hydroelectric power to run all of the canal's functions, including the locomotive that is used to tow the ships through the locks. Because a prolonged drought could deplete Gatun Lake, the canal planners added Madden Lake as a supplementary water source.

At Culebra, east of Gatun Lake, the project encountered its most formidable challenge—cutting an eight-mile-long passage through the backbone of the Americas and across the Continental Divide. To prepare the route through an area of extremely unstable terrain, workers unleashed a total force of 61 million pounds of dynamite, which exceeded the total explosive power used in all of the wars before that time. Excavation of the Culebra (later called Gaillard) Cut subjected engineers and workers to temperatures of 130°F and made them vulnerable to frequent rock and mud slides. After one landslide wiped out months of work, an undaunted Goethals responded, "Hell, dig it out again!" Eventually, he ordered the cut flooded because dredging would be faster and less expensive than re-digging.

Just past the cut, the Pedro Miguel and Miraflores Locks lower southbound ships to the level of the Pacific Ocean in two stages. From Miraflores, ships pass through the remaining eight miles of channel and into the sea.

The construction of the Panama Canal lasted 10 years, cost 387 million dollars, and moved enough earth to build 63 piles the size of the Great Pyramid of Khufu. It united the world's great oceans and thrust the United States into a global leadership role just as World War I was beginning to change the course of the century.

Tight fit: An electric tug on tracks tows a large cargo ship through Miraflores Locks near the canal's Pacific side. The Panama locks' 110-foot width precludes passage of supertankers and supercarriers.

The Channel Tunnel

··········

Modern Wonders

Behemoth at rest, a tunnel boring machine—one of 11 designed to excavate the chalk marl of the English Channel seabed—takes a break during construction of the Channel Tunnel.

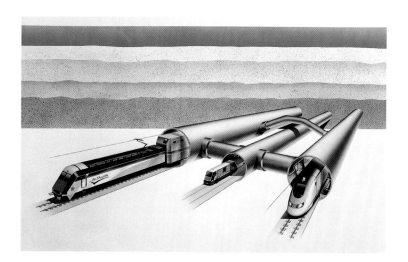

For more than two centuries the French said, "Oui, oui!" and the English replied, "No, no!" The idea of a tunnel under the English Channel, regardless of its practicality, did not appeal to the insular English. They feared the French would use it for nefarious purposes, such as an invasion, or for less nefarious purposes, perhaps adding a continental touch to English cuisine—the "garlic factor," as some wags asserted. In recent decades, opposition to a Channel tunnel was encompassed by the larger issue of reluctance to become part of a European union.

Sleek design of the Channel Tunnel (top) contrasts sharply with the crude undersea avenue of invasion conjured up in this 1803 French engraving (above).

Rotating tungsten teeth (right) chewed through the Channel's bedrock at the rate of 15 feet an hour.

In fairness, the tunnel idea did have some English proponents, including Queen Victoria, who supported the building of a tunnel because it would provide an alternative to surface crossings in rough weather. Though smallish as bodies of water go, the Channel is swept by gale-force winds about once a week. During the Victorian era, numerous tunnel schemes were proposed, some of which involved sunken tubes and such ventilating devices as floating pavilions. Test digging actually took place in the late 1870s and early 1880s.

Ultimately, French insistence overcame English resistance. In 1986, British Prime Minister Margaret Thatcher and French President François Mitterrand announced the signing of an agreement to allow tunnel legislation to proceed. The project would be an Anglo-French venture, administered jointly by an entity called Eurotunnel and built by an Anglo-French consortium of contractors called Transmanche Link. (La Manche, or "the sleeve," is the French name for the Channel.) Funding, which came entirely from the private sector, involved 225 banks from 26 nations. The French maintained their proactive approach, outnumbering British stockholders four to one.

The Channel Tunnel, or "Chunnel," is really three tunnels in one, running 31 miles from a terminal in Folkestone, England, to another in Coquelles, France. Two main tunnels almost 25 feet in diameter are designed to carry cars, buses, passengers, and trucks on high-speed shuttles; they also can carry through-trains. In between is a smaller service tunnel. Linked by cross passages to the rail tunnels, it allows for emergency responses, evacuations, maintenance, and fresh air. There is also a "crossover canyon," 70 feet wide and 30 feet high, where the two rail tunnels merge. Here, trains can move from one tunnel to the other, if necessary. The surface of the Channel bears no evidence of the Chunnel: Its 24 underwater miles lie 130 feet beneath the seabed.

Underwater tunneling carries inherent risks of cave in and flooding. But in 1825, undersea tunneling became much safer when British engineer Marc Isambard Brunel developed a new kind of tunnel boring machine (TBM). Encased in a shield, it protected the operators and held up tunnel walls until linings could be installed. His TBM was first used successfully in the Thames River Tunnel.

The machines that would tackle the tunneling under the English Channel were thousand-ton behemoths known by numbers on the English side and by women's names on the French. The Chunnel TBMs could not only cut through the soft chalk marl layer of the channel bed, but they could also dispose of the spoil and install sections of tunnel lining. The marvelous machines could do just about everything but make lunch for the workers.

Tunneling began on both sides of the Channel in 1987. The English started from the shore at Shakespeare Cliff, near Dover, while the French constructed a shaft at Sangatte, near Calais, into which they lowered their TBMs. To set and keep the tunnel ends in alignment, surveyors started out by using such traditional methods as triangulation, plumb lines, and dead reckoning. But inside the tunnel, they were guided by TBM computers and laser beams. When at last the time came for the first undersea breakthrough—in the service tunnel on December 1, 1990—the alignment of the tunnel sections was found to be within a few centimeters. It was an amazing feat.

During work on the Chunnel, the TBMs used rotary disks equipped with sharp tungsten teeth to chew away the marl. As the machines advanced, chunks of marl were passed back to the shaft openings via conveyor belts and rolling carts. In both England and France, the marl was used to form artificial lagoons close to the construction sites. These areas were eventually filled in and covered with vegetation.

Like all tunnels, the Channel Tunnel must address important issues of safety and environmental health. To cope with vehicular exhaust, much shorter tunnels use fan systems that rely on fresh air from each end. The Chunnel's length precludes this option; there is no satisfactory way for a 31-mile-long tunnel to remove fumes and recirculate the air. For this reason, specially built electric trains carry all traffic. Fourteen feet across, they are the largest train-wagons ever built. Cars and buses drive onto loading platforms and then onto the double-deck trains. The electric trains create no pollution, but they do require a cooling system. To this end, cold-water piping totaling 340 miles in length runs along the tracks. The tunnel's design also includes drainage pumps that deal with rainwater and water seepage.

The Channel Tunnel was completed in 1994 at a cost of 13.5 billion dollars. Since then, passenger traffic on Le Shuttle, as the high-speed trains are called, has tended to be rather lopsided. As it turns out, the English heading for France and the delights of the Continent outnumber the French traveling to England and points north. The shore-to-shore part of the journey takes a mere 35 minutes, and the route from London to Paris is only some three hours long. Queen Victoria would be happy.

In London, Eurostar trains wait for Paris-bound passengers at Waterloo Station's recently renovated international terminal. After a comfortable, three-hour journey aboard one of the high-speed trains, passengers can set foot on French soil.

The North Sea Protection Works

··········

Modern Wonders

Poised for action, 31 gates span the two northern channels of the Oosterschelde barrier. Completed in 1986, the barrier helps safeguard the Netherlands from powerful North Sea surges.

To prevent seabed erosion at the base of a dam enclosing the former Zuider Zee, Dutch workers in the 1920s used rocks to sink mattresses made of brushwood (right).

In the aftermath of a severe 1953 storm, river waters breached a dike (below) at a southern Netherlands town—27 miles from the North Sea.

For many, the image of the Dutch fight against the North Sea rests in the figure of a young boy valiantly saving his town by using a finger to plug a hole in a dike. But this familiar hero is a fictional one, a creation of American author Mary Mapes Dodge in her book, *Hans Brinker*. In reality, heroism falls on all the Dutch, who for more than a millennium have been wresting precious agricultural lands from the sea and fighting to hold onto them. Their greatest achievement—a colossal thumb in the dike—is the vast and wondrous project known as the Netherlands North Sea Protection Works.

Because much of the Netherlands lies below sea level, normal tides would daily inundate about half the country if previous generations of industrious Dutch had not raised dikes and dams. Severe storms often cause tidal waters to crash into the dikes and inundate rivers and estuaries. Although all of the coastal areas are threatened, two particularly vulnerable ones are the large tidal inlet formerly known as the Zuider Zee and the delta created by the Rhine and Meuse Rivers in the southwestern corner of the country.

Dutch engineers first proposed that the Zuider Zee be dammed and drained in the 19th century, but the government was reluctant to tackle such an immense project. Then, in 1916, a furious storm hit the northern

To help carry out the Delta Plan, the *Cardium* groomed the floor of the Oosterschelde estuary before unrolling 5,500-ton mattresses to stabilize it.

provinces. The difficulties of wartime agricultural production were compounded, and the way was paved for the damming of the Zuider Zee.

The dam enclosing the Zuider Zee was built in two sections using traditional materials. Beginning in 1923, workers laid boulder clay in parallel layers and filled the space in between with sand, stones, and handmade mattresses fashioned from brushwood. To curtail erosion, larger mattresses ballasted with chains and stones were sunk in the estuary's channels. Dredges, cranes, tugboats, and barges were engaged in the erection of the main dam, 300 feet wide at sea level and 25 feet high at the level of its causeway. As the tide turned on the final day of construction, fill tumbled into the dam's last gap, transforming the inlet into a freshwater lake, renamed the Ijsselmeer. The finished dam contained sluices for draining excess water and locks for maintaining shipping.

After the damming came the draining. In all, more than a half million acres of polders, or reclaimed farmland, emerged from the bottom of the former Zuider Zee. Young Dutch farmers clamored for the right to settle the new polder lands, because farms on new, unobstructed land were far more suitable for modern, mechanized farming methods than traditional farms in older areas.

In 1953, the "storm of the century" howled across the North Sea and into the Netherlands, testing the strength of the Zuider Zee enclosure. It held, with damage to the causeway heavy in places. The country's unprotected southwestern provinces felt the full brunt of the storm, with water surging over seawalls and up the delta's wide

To build the Oosterschelde barrier, 18,000-ton concrete piers (below) constructed on docks below sea level eliminated the need for costly cofferdams. Gantry cranes on the *Ostrea* (right) lift a pier from an intentionally flooded dock. Positioned in the estuary, piers support the barrier's sea gates and roadway (far right).

waterways. More than 1,800 people lost their lives, and livestock numbering in the hundreds of thousands perished. The country then realized that the long-intended plan to safeguard the southwestern delta, the Delta Plan or Delta Project, must be mobilized.

The plan would undergo many incarnations. The last one involved damming four estuaries in the middle of the delta while leaving open channels to Rotterdam in the north and Antwerp, Belgium, in the south. A two-mile-long surge barrier in the Oosterschelde estuary was the most complex and sophisticated piece of the project.

Originally, the Oosterschelde was to be a closed barrier. But lobbying by fishermen and conservationists resulted in the switch to a movable barrier. To facilitate construction, engineers fashioned islands on three sandbars in the estuary and constructed work harbors, material yards, and work sites there. A dam connected two of the islands, effectively creating three channels in the estuary, each to receive a section of the surge barrier.

The movable barrier consists of 65 concrete piers weighing 18,000 tons apiece. The piers support 300- to 500-ton steel gates and their hydraulic machinery, as

well as a roadway above and load-bearing beams below. Constructed on the work islands, the piers and their mechanisms had to be lifted into precise positions in the estuary. But the type of equipment needed for such gargantuan and specialized tasks did not exist anywhere in the world; it had to be invented.

The Oosterschelde barrier also honored traditional methods. As part of the measures taken to stabilize the seafloor, mattresses were laid under each pier to prevent erosion. They were not the hand-built weavings of trees and brush used to close the Zuider Zee, however. Instead,

they were high-tech sandwiches of sand and gravel between space-age fabric covers. The Oosterschelde project was finished in 1986. Since then, the Dutch have taken additional measures, including the completion in 1997 of a barrier that protects the port of Rotterdam.

"In terms of magnitude," an American trade journal wrote, the North Sea project "approaches the Great Wall of China. In terms of complexity and technical sophistication, it approaches a lunar space shot. It is unique, expensive, and quite unlike any other civil engineering project to be found on this planet."

The Golden Gate Bridge

··········

Modern Wonders

High above San Francisco Bay, pedestri-
ans jam the Golden Gate Bridge during
Bridgewalk '87. They echo the day, 50
years earlier, when strollers got first
run of the new suspension bridge.

When a heavy fog shrouds the base of its steel towers, the main span of the Golden Gate Bridge seems to be suspended in midair like some celestial conjurer's trick. The illusion is apt, because it took a kind of conjuring to build the bridge that many qualified critics said could never be built.

The 19th-century explorer John C. Frémont named the Golden Gate passage as an analogue to the ancient harbor of Byzantium, the Golden Horn. Nearly a mile wide, this break in northern California's coastline is a zone of forceful tides and capricious currents that grow stronger during frequent high winds and storms.

The need for a bridge spanning the Golden Gate follows the history of the city once known as Yerba Buena. A sleepy fort and mission founded in 1776, the village of Yerba Buena became an 1849 Gold Rush city of 35,000 people and was renamed San Francisco. Towns soon rimmed the perimeter of the bay, including the rugged peninsula on the north side of the Gate. For decades, travelers to San Francisco from the bay's north shore were content to take a ferry across. But the advent of the automobile and its sidekick, the traffic jam, soon led to discussions about building a bridge.

In 1916, a commuting journalist began an editorial campaign and sketched out a plan that bore an uncanny resemblance to the bridge built 21 years later. Chicago engineer Joseph Strauss, who had patented a kind of cantilever structure but had never built a suspension bridge, also championed the Golden Gate project. Despite the practicality of a span over the Golden Gate, the public response was mixed. Objections surfaced from the Navy and War Departments, which feared the curtailment of military operations; from ferry and railroad operators, who risked losing passengers; and from timber barons, who feared "an infusion of flatlanders and tourists."

All of these obstacles and the 1929 stock market crash combined to hold up funding for the bridge for almost a decade. Finally, with a bond floated by the Bank of America (now a landmark itself on the San Francisco skyline), the project began to go forward. The bridge-to-be would have a main span of 4,200 feet and side spans of 1,125 feet. The cables were to be drawn over two 746-foot steel towers, a record height that still holds. They would be secured into eyebars locked into 60,000-ton anchorages on land at each end of the bridge. Suspenders, or hangers, would run from the main cable to the bridge floor.

Geology reports brought the good news that an underwater rock ledge could support the bridge's north pier and tower. Unfortunately, construction of the south pier and tower would prove to be more challenging. They would have to be built 1,100 feet offshore in a channel with an average depth of 100 feet and tides of about 7 knots. Therein lay the supreme challenge: No bridge pier had ever been constructed in the open sea.

Construction of the anchorages began in 1933. After the excavation of enormous pits, concrete reinforced with steel and manufactured on-site was poured in. The concrete buried the steel eyebars, leaving only the ends

Temporary footbridges hang from the completed bridge towers in preparation for cabling. Cables spun on-site followed their path up and over the towers and down to the anchorages on land.

showing. The anchorages would ultimately bear responsibility for the bridge's nearly 250 million pounds of dead and live load.

The north tower, on its rocky platform, was started next. Workers first secured a dry work site by building a three-sided cofferdam and then pumping it out. While the north tower was completed ahead of schedule, the south

tower had a difficult beginning. The plan was to build a wharf out to the site. But before the wharf could be put into service, its concrete fender suffered a triple indignity. A freighter rammed it and two storms tore it apart.

To dig and sink the south tower's pier, workers first had to erect an elliptical cofferdam the size of a football field in open water. The work was hazardous, with divers in the bay having only 20 minutes of slack water four times a day in which to accomplish it. Once this work got going, though, construction of the south tower proceeded more or less without incident.

When the tower piers were finished, Bethlehem Steel began shipping steel from the East through the Panama Canal. Local crews of fearless ironworkers were hired, and derricks and rigs that had been used to build New York's George Washington Bridge were brought in. Cabling work was the responsibility of John Roebling and Sons, builders of the Brooklyn Bridge. Roebling adapted the on-site cable spinning methods used earlier, sending cold-drawn steel wire on rollers up and over the towers, down to the anchorages, and back again—enough wire to travel the Equator three times. When the thick bundles of wire

reached a yard in diameter they were compressed by a hydraulic jack, banded with cast-steel clamps, and wrapped in a layer of fine wire. With cabling completed, only the work on the bridge floor and roadway remained.

Opening ceremonies on May 27, 1937, began with a mass pedestrian crossing. Now painted a striking international orange, the Golden Gate Bridge shimmered in the light as adults and children raced gleefully across the wide span. In his official remarks, designer Strauss called his magnum opus "a giant portal that seems like a mighty door, swinging wide into a world of wonder."

With a grace belying its strength, the Golden Gate Bridge frames the city of San Francisco. After a section of the San Francisco-Oakland Bay Bridge collapsed in a 1989 earthquake, engineers scrambled to find ways to prevent such a disaster from occurring at the Golden Gate. They began a painstaking reinforcement program to protect the magnificent structure from future earthquakes.

Library of Congress ℭℙ Data

The wonders of the world / prepared by the Book Division, National Geographic Society.
        p.   cm.
      Includes index.
      ISBN 0-7922-7200-5 (reg). —ISBN 0-7922-7201-3 (dlx)
        1. Landforms. 2. Natural monuments. 3. Seven Wonders of the World.
    I. National Geographic Society (U.S.). Book Division.
    GB406.W66 1998
    031.02—dc21   98-11976
                                                    ℭℙ

Composition for this book by the National Geographic Society Book Division. Color separations by Quad Graphics, Martinsburg, West Virginia. Printed and bound by R. R. Donnelley & Sons, Willard, Ohio. Dust jacket printed by Miken, Inc., Cheektowaga, New York.

Visit the Society's Web site at www.nationalgeographic.com.